YOU CAN BEGIN IMMEDIATELY
TO PERFORM MIRACLES IN EVERY AREA OF YOUR LIFE

• *Attract money,* not because you are greedy, but because life doesn't have to be a struggle. Discover the means to release yourself from a work-hard-to-achieve mentality and start now to enjoy the wealth and abundance you're entitled to and deserve.

• *Take care of the real and pressing needs in your life* and along the way, explore your inner gifts and the dynamic energy of your higher mind. Live your dreams and let your desires lead you to the greatest and most sublime spiritual awareness.

• *Discover the natural creative power within you,* which you can use to control the conditions of your life and, ultimately, your destiny. Many people go through life and never know the power they have to turn what they think into reality. Discover for yourself the remarkable power within you and a life filled with more happiness, meaning, passion and joy.

• *Learn how to dream in such a way that what you hold in your mind will manifest in the outer world* as the people, events and things you want in your life. Discover the creative principles that make this possible and share in the stories of so many people who have created wealth, happiness, healing and success.

• *Achieve greater health and increase your energy.* Everyday, we experience the body's reactions to our emotions and imagined fears. Learn through this Practice to harness the powerful energy of your thoughts and heal your mind and body and bring strength to yourself and others.

• *Enjoy the positive gifts in life* and receive love, pleasure, praise and admiration. Come to fully expect and truly believe in something far greater for your life. Watch as your surroundings begin to magically reflect back to you what you are now willing to give to yourself.

• *Create a map of your soul* and use it to alter the way you perceive your life. Discover the world through the eyes of your soul and naturally attract an abundant and rewarding life.

• *Discover the secrets to "one-pointed" thought* and learn how you can overcome unhappiness, anxiety, guilt, doubt and fear. Often in life, our consciousness is like a magnet struck too many times and it loses its ability to attract to the positive rewards in life. You can learn to recharge your mind and magnetize your life to attract the positive experiences you desire.

• *Start today to sleep better* and make your hours of rest work to your benefit. Program your mind to carry the pleasurable images of your desires into your sleep and transform your nighttime dreams into powerful tools that speed the realization of your desires.

• *Overcome loneliness* and experience a sense of wholeness. Learn of your connection to all things and how it gives you your natural power of creation.

• *Feel comfortable in your own skin.* As you cultivate your inner gifts, you will become more intuitive and express yourself more freely. You will experience a renewed sense of self-mastery and confidence and naturally attract the people and social circumstances you desire and that benefit your life.

• *Do you want to lose weight? Stop smoking? Improve your life and change negative habits?* Over time, our ability to choose becomes less of a deliberate act and more of an automatic habit of will. Learn the formula that creates your will and re-program your mind to automatically think, feel and act in positive ways.

• *Find out what you want in life.* Discover your talents and passion and begin to live and work to share your unique expression with others.

• *Receive the answers to life's questions.* Come to know who you truly are and understand the existence you find yourself in.

• *Study the SIX SIMPLE STEPS that turn dreams and wishes into reality.* There is a wonder and excitement in your heart and mind that will recreate the conditions of your life. Now is the time to let your inner gifts shine brilliantly into the world. Now is the perfect time.

PROFESSIONAL
dreamer

6 Simple Steps that turn Dreams into Reality

ghalil

One Mind
Publishing

Copyright ©2005 by Ghalil.
2nd Printing.

Library and Archives Canada Cataloguing in Publication Data
Ghalil, 1968-
Professional dreamer : learn to use the powerful energy of your thoughts to manifest the life you want : 6 simple steps that turn dreams into reality / Ghalil.

ISBN 0-9736894-0-4
1. Self-actualization (Psychology) I. Title.
BF637.S4.G478 2005 158.1   C2005-901416-4

One Mind Publishing
http:/www.onemindpublishing.com

Cover design and layout by Jacqueline Verkley
Edited by Marial Shea

Printed in Canada

For the one who reads this now, please know that I offer this as an expression of love to take into your life—from now and on....

CONTENTS

TO MY READERS

Have you ever wondered why some people seem to easily attract rewards and happiness, while others struggle to take one small step forward only to be thrown three steps back?

I wondered. I spent the better (worse) part of my life as a successful mess: an overly sensitive, workaholic worrywart who, ironically, taught wildly successful seminars and workshops in the area of personal growth. Imagine! Mind you, my success was likely due to my sincere empathy and passion, because more than anything, I was trying to teach myself.

To this end, I eagerly listened to the experience of others, immersed myself in various teachings and traditions, attended different churches, practiced Buddhism, contorted my body, lied to myself with affirmations and positive thinking, meditated, chanted, visualized and prayed.

In the end, I seemed to know very clearly what I should be doing, but I didn't exactly know how to do it. I understood: *the only reality is the one in our minds.* But knowing this, I still hadn't found the key to change my reality once and for all. And I can't say I was completely convinced that my thoughts alone had the power to change my reality. There certainly seemed to be "fates" conspiring to make my journey a difficult one.

Then, I became ill. For the first time in my life, I couldn't work. For a year, things in my life deteriorated and slipped away: my health, relationship, career. Eventually, I ran out of money and all I could think was that, after trying so hard, I had only made it as far as square one.

And so, one night, I gave in. I didn't give up. I knew there was an answer. I think that, deep down, we all know there's an answer, something more to all this. But, I decided to let the answer find me.

Looking back, it was in that moment that I declared myself worthy. In that moment, I finally believed I could receive something without struggle, sweat or payment.

That night, I pulled myself out of bed, headed into the kitchen to make tea, and froze. Even though I was alone, I had the distinct feeling someone called my name. Then a thought entered my mind as clearly as if it were being spoken, *"You're everything you need to be and everything you need is in you."* And information flooded my mind, much of which I don't recall ever knowing and most of it astonished me. The information was presented as if in a painting, where I could perceive everything on the canvas at once. In that moment, I understood us—collectively—as a creative force and I knew how to cultivate this power.

I believe I accessed information we all share. And I also like to think that, perhaps, after twenty years of sharing every insight I've gleaned, I've been given a greater responsibility.

What I can tell you for sure is that the information I witnessed left me with two things: the knowledge to manifest, in each moment, the conditions I want in my life, and a gnawing urgency to share the information.

I first told a small group of people and, within days, received numerous phone calls and emails, some from people I had never met, telling me of "unbelievable" and "miraculous" changes in their lives. From then on, I was drawn to others for whom it seemed the material was specifically intended. Soon, I was meeting with people every day. Eventually, someone asked if I would condense the information into a book. Curiously, the moment I put pen to paper the feeling of urgency left me.

The book in your hands is the first segment of the information presented to me, a first step in a much greater spiritual journey. It is intended to give you necessary control of your thoughts and, thus, your energy.

Professional Dreamer focuses on the creation of form so that you can clearly and concretely witness the effects of your thoughts and energy. Indeed, you exist in part on a physical level specifically for this purpose, to witness the effects of your thoughts so that you may learn to think properly.

On a higher level of energy, there is no interval of time between what you think and the creation of form. But on the physical level it takes some time for thought to evolve to a material level. Here, you have time to observe the cause and effect relationship. Thus, you can learn to control your thoughts—your creations and, ultimately, your contributions to all.

Initially, you are encouraged to take care of your physical needs and wants, because the physical world is what we know well. Our material desires are things we are familiar with. And it's always easiest to start with what we know and slowly move into the unknown.

I welcome you to this book. I know, with a deep certainty, it was intended for you. This information has found you, as it did me, which means that somewhere along the way you opened the door to let more into your life.

Certainly, you will find much of the "translator" in this work, but you will also pick up on much that lies beyond the writing, as this is only a vehicle through which a greater energy will reach you.

I invite you now to explore this book. I consider it to be a layperson's manual for using the most powerful tool we possess: our mind. I believe you'll recognize much of the information as what you already know to be true within you. I also believe it will dramatically change your life for the better, and when it does, I know that through you, the information will reach all those for whom it is intended, in just the right way, at the right time.

Soon, every ear will be readied to hear something much greater and we'll all live, as we truly are…joyous.

The stories within are presented with permission.

No problem can be solved from the same level of consciousness that created it. We must learn to see the world anew.
—Albert Einstein

I now open my heart and mind.
Oh, what I had not seen before rushes my soul,
filling me with an erupting exhuberance.
I open my tingling fingers,
my palms fill with a weighty abundance.
Oh, what I now see.
Divine radiating light,
surrounds me, fills my heart and mind, wells within me.
I see my connection to all things.
I feel all things a part of me.
I am as a beacon.
Everything I could ever want is seeking me now.

introduction

This book is written to show you that you are so much more powerful than you may realize. You have within you the power to create, which you extend with every thought. Every time you think, you bring into existence a new and unique creation—as real as a bridge or building. Thought has its own materialization. It has substance. And although it may not be immediately apparent, you have the power to bring your thoughts to a physical level of materialization.

This book is written to show you how thought evolves from the inner world of mind to the outer world of physical reality. Further, it gives you the practical means, in the form of six simple steps, to quickly and effectively harness the power of thought so you can consistently create the experiences and conditions you want to have in this lifetime. You can think and create money, attract love, heal your mind and body, feel truly confident, happy, energized and fulfilled and find the peace and security you deserve. You can manifest all that you may want or need…when you once discover the concrete reality of your thoughts.

Thoughts Are Things

Your thoughts are far more than just ideas and images that pass through your mind and drive your words and actions. Thoughts are things, as real and permanent as this book in your hands.

Thought is energy, a fine, vibratory and highly changeable form of energy. Just as your heart beats all day and all night and generates a measurable field of electromagnetic energy, so, too, you think all day

3

and all night and generate a powerful field of mental energy—the same subtle substance, the same raw material that creates the concrete things in your life.

All things are manifestations of energy. Everything we taste, touch, hear, smell and see, and everything we don't see, is energy. The energy in a book is simply of a quality slow enough, dense enough and stable enough for us to perceive it with our senses. But as we move away from physical matter to higher levels, energy becomes less detectable. Air is a finer and more mobile form of energy and therefore less perceptible. Magnetism and gravity are forms of energy almost completely beyond our physical apprehension. The fact that we can't see energy on one level doesn't argue its existence. Everything is energy.

It's hardly surprising then to discover that thought, like everything, is energy. And all of what you experience is simply the same subtle substance that has sufficiently condensed, or collected together, to evolve to a perceptible level.

The subtle substance of your innermost dreams and wishes can be easily evolved to manifest on a material level.

Why, then, can it happen that things we wish for do not translate to the level of physical reality? Because we don't often think in the same manner as we would if we were constructing something with our hands, consciously moulding and directing the substance of our thoughts. We tend to regard thought as something we do, not some *thing* that we can use to create the material conditions of our life.

> We tend to regard thought as something we do, not some *thing* that we can use to create the material conditions of our life.

When you form and hold a thought in your mind, you are creating it, just as if you were constructing it with your hands. And in the same way, it takes concentration and imagination to plan and chart the details of your creation. It also takes a measure of time to assemble the elements of creation—all of which must have a purpose and place in the construction of your desire. If you were constructing a house you wouldn't gather together the materials to build a barn.

And yet, this is how we think much of the time. Not every thought has a purpose in our plan. Our thoughts wander and see-saw between this and that. One thought contradicts the next. We think about what we *don't* want as much, if not more, as we think about what we *do* want. Simply, we tend to think in a disorganized and cluttered manner and produce energy too weak and ineffective to manifest in familiar form.

As well, a generally chaotic manner of thought makes us receptive to the energy around us such that we can spend the better part of our lives twisting and turning in response to the whims of others. And in the absence of a steady stream of productive thought, it's easy for the well-practiced emotions of fear, limitation and regret to take the place of specific, conscious desire and dictate the conditions of our lives.

Occasionally, however, we inadvertently produce desirable results and catch a glimpse of our power, experiencing what seem to be coincidences, luck, miracles and random occurrences. It's often at odd times, when we're relaxed and hold in our mind a single, clear, uncomplicated thought. We might think about a song we love, and for a moment nothing else occupies our mind, and suddenly, the song plays on the radio. We might start thinking about someone we haven't seen in years until they're all we can think about, and they call within moments. Or, we feel urged to walk into a place we had no intention of visiting and find just the thing we had been daydreaming about only minutes before.

If there is only one thing that is important to understand, it is that every thought is potentially creative. If you guard what you allow to occupy your mind, you can control the conditions of your life and, ultimately, your destiny.

To be clearer, and to show you just how readily you can transform your thinking and achieve miraculous results, let me share with you one woman's story.

CLARA'S STORY

Like many of us, Clara came about the *Practice* described for you in this book at a time of great need. She had left a marriage of almost twenty years, moved to a new city, knew no one and, within days, became gravely ill. Her body was ravaged by a host of ailments and she found it almost impossible to move without considerable pain. She visited numerous doctors and specialists who diagnosed everything from cholesterol and ulcers to fibromyalgia.

Unable to work, Clara relied on charity. She never had more than fifty dollars to her name and very little else. She lived in motel after motel, and finally, an old, sparsely furnished bachelor suite. The carpets were worn through; there were no knickknacks or decorations, only a bed, chair and two mismatched end tables.

For three years, Clara was confined to this suite, where her life seemed to be one long struggle to get out of bed. Every afternoon, she awoke feeling tired and stiff and coaxed herself to reach for a glass of water and medication. She would then lie perfectly still, staring at a water-stained ceiling, while she waited patiently for the first of several drugs to ease the pain in her arms and legs. She would eventually force herself to get up and make toast, an exercise that would take a little over twenty minutes and leave her completely exhausted.

After three and a half years and no improvement, Clara met me. I shared with her the steps in this book, which she immediately put into practise. In her thoughts, she took up living her life exactly as she wanted it to be. She created a picture in her mind of her health and what she saw as her best life, and this vision became her only focus. It never occurred to Clara that it might not work or that she was simply trying yet another doomed-to-fail remedy. In her mind, she wasn't dreaming; she was designing an interesting life.

Six weeks later, Clara awoke one morning and was completely fine. That afternoon, she began a new project, which she later invited me to see. On the wall beside her bed, she had created a visual representation of her new desires. She had taped up six pictures.

The first picture had been cut from a magazine. It showed a loving couple with the word "magic" scrolled across the top. Along the bottom it read, "And just like that…it begins."

The second picture was a car. Clara had never had a car and she didn't drive, but she said that she would take driving lessons as soon as she got the car.

The third picture was of a large and obviously imitation check for a million dollars made out in her name, which Clara explained had come with one of those mail-in contests. It had arrived just as she was adding the idea of money to her life so, "Why not!" she said, suggesting that a million dollars was as good a sum as any to start with.

The fourth image was the front of a card that read "celebrate" and showed a woman laughing. Clara explained that this picture was the epitome of life for her, and that she would celebrate every day.

The fifth picture was taken from the balcony of a palatial home and showed a beautiful beach. Clara had decided that she would live in a place such as this with a large swimming pool. She explained to me that, shortly after she taped the picture to the wall, she was asked to someone's house that had a pool very much like she desired. She immediately asked the owner for a photo and displayed it above her own cut-out picture in a seashell embossed frame.

As Clara set the frame back in its place, I noticed that she spoke of and handled each picture with great care. For Clara, these pictures were pregnant with possibility and she was nurturing them until they were ready to be born.

The final photo was tiny. It had been carefully traced with scissors and taped to the corner of the imitation check. It showed a Yorkshire terrier. When I pointed this out, Clara just smiled, closed her eyes and slowly nodded. She had thought of every detail.

Clara then showed me a journal filled with notes about her life. She had written pages and pages about her lover—all the things he said and what he gave her, in the exact order she desired. In Clara's mind, everything had already happened.

Clara then threw her hands in the air and declared that, since it was all too much to remember, she had condensed her desires into one sentence. Her face lit up and, with incredible excitement, she said, "I woke up the other day and decided that life begins at fifty." This was her sentence. All that she had destined would take place when she turned fifty, less than two months away.

Clara then opened her wallet and withdrew a newspaper clipping. It was a horoscope and reminded, "Your life is just beginning." Every day, she looked at it and spoke these words out loud.

Clara never questioned the reality of such a dream. If anyone asked her how she knew without any doubt that all this was going to happen, she simply looked back at them perplexed. Clara couldn't understand such questions. She simply couldn't fathom any doubt. In response, she would point to her pictures and tell everyone to look at all that she was soon going to have. And then she would quickly change the subject, turning to new ideas and greater plans.

Not long after, about three weeks from the time she completed her collage, Clara was out for a walk and wandered into a used bookstore. Thumbing through an old magazine, she discovered a used airline ticket and boarding pass folded together and tucked between two pages. Clara suddenly had the idea to write her name on both and add them to her collage. She called me to say that she had just had the inspiration to travel and couldn't believe her luck to have found an old ticket that, in her words, obviously made travel possible.

The next day, Clara was asked to dinner by an elderly couple who lived nearby. The couple had heard through neighbors that Clara was out of work and hoped she might agree to accompany them on a long flight and cruise. They knew that Clara had little money and offered to finance her spending. Clara agreed. The arrangements were made and off she went.

After several days, she called to say that her companions were content to stay in their cabin. She told me that she was beginning to feel lonely. However, without a further hint of displeasure, she informed me that she would speak to the cruise director and try and find some activities to fill her time.

She never made it to the director. She met a man who spoke to her exactly as she had decided in her plan. She arrived home, staying only long enough to say goodbye. She was marrying this man. She left the day after her fiftieth birthday.

She now enjoys a gorgeous mansion with a lovely pool; a million dollars, a car and, of course, driving lessons. She celebrates every day and each moment is magic. And at night when she rests, a sweet Yorkshire terrier curls up in her lap.

WHAT ARE YOU WILLING TO ACCEPT?

Thought is powerful. What you think creates your life. All you have to do is ask yourself what you are willing to accept into your life and learn to focus your thoughts to consciously and consistently create what you want.

This book will show you how to create a clear and consistent pattern of thought to release your full creative potential and achieve a fuller, better life.

Professional Dreaming is the skilful application of thought to manifest objective reality. It's about learning how to dream in such a way that what you hold in your mind will manifest in the outer world as the people, events and things you want in your life.

Professional Dreamer combines the constructs of science with the principles and teachings of metaphysics to give you the keys to mental creation in one simple, practical, easy-to-follow book. It clearly tells you what to think and how to think to manifest the life you want.

As this book has found you, know that you have the ability, the willingness and the readiness for something much greater in your life. We each find the key when the time is right, and it comes with such force, and so convincingly, that we cannot help but see it. The most wondrous and sublime experiences await you.

Take this book. Study it. Refer to it, as you need. Let it bring you the life of your dreams—or rather, let your dreams bring you a richer, healthier, more abundant life!

six simple steps

AN OVERVIEW

I took six steps and turned around and found no road behind me.
I quickly turned and looked ahead and found no road before me.
I closed my eyes into a dream and found a world inside me.
And when I chose to look again, my dreams were all around me.

I am now in the consciousness of good.
I know only good.
My thoughts are good.
My dreams are good.
My body knows only good.
I feel good.
I give good.
Only good returns to me.
I am a loving, trusting child of perfect goodness.
I am good.

SIX SIMPLE STEPS
AN OVERVIEW

Described for you here is the *Practice:* a repeatable sequence of *six simple steps* that ultimately form a habit. The Practice is not concepts and ideas that you have to remind yourself to contemplate throughout the day, rather each step clearly tells you what to *do*, minute to minute.

This overview will give you the opportunity to see the Practice as one complete picture. In fact, think of the Practice as a recipe—for all the experiences and conditions you want in your life. It clearly tells you what ingredients you need and how to mix them to achieve the life you want.

In total, there are six ingredients—six simple steps—that turn dreams into material fact. When studied and practised, these steps assemble your thoughts, emotions and actions so that you can exert control over the conditions of your life and live the dreams you desire.

THE PRACTICE

STEP ONE ~ One-Pointed Thought
DEVELOP AND MAINTAIN ONE-POINTED THOUGHT

One-pointed thought is pure or uncluttered thought. It is a dynamic, consistent way of thinking, free of negativity and thoughts in opposition to your desires.

You can begin now to align your thoughts with one-pointed thinking. Think of your every thought as an arrow. When you "nok" an arrow (fit it to its string) it's because you intend to use it. Fit your thoughts to a definite and dynamic purpose. Of course, for an arrow of thought to reach its target its pathway must be clear.

Therefore, your first step is to clearly identify your mental clutter, which is all of your repeating negative, distracting, aimless, competitive and contradictory thoughts that systematically impede the flow of positive and productive mental energy.

Simply, clutter does what clutter does. It litters your mind and disorganizes your thoughts so that the energy you produce is too weak and ineffective to manifest in material form.

Step One will take you through the creation of your own *Inventory Journal*, a quick, easy and practical way to clear your mind of clutter and establish a habitual pattern of positive, singular focus in preparation for the steps that follow.

Step One also involves an exercise in *Clearing*, which is the physical compliment to mental clearing. It will cleanse your environment of the physical matter that can have an effect as disruptive as mental clutter.

> Think of your every thought as an expertly aimed arrow.

Clearing will invite an incredible influx of energy into your life. It will instantly give you the same sensation you want to experience when you think creatively. And it is a ritual of commitment, wherein you acknowledge your gifts and prepare to accept a greater life for yourself.

STEP TWO ~ Desire

DISCOVER AND EXPLORE YOUR DESIRE

In this step, you will discover your *desire*, which is what you truly want to experience in your life, *right now.* Desire gives your thoughts a focus—a target to which you'll aim every arrow of thought.

You can start even now to organize your thoughts around ideas and images of things, people and events that you would love to experience *right now.* Start reasonably. Focus on things you *do* believe and *can* expect for yourself.

Desire will assist you to quickly and effectively control your thoughts. Whenever negativity arises, thoughts in opposition to your desire erupt or you become distracted in any way, you can restore yourself by picturing your objective and focusing solely on your desire.

Desire assembles your thoughts and energy into a clear pattern, a sort of energized blueprint, which, in turn, assembles the energy around you, moulding and shaping it to eventually form as the things you think about.

Step Two will bring you to discover your desires and to narrow your focus if you have conflicting interests or feel that there are too many things you desire all at once.

In *Step Two* you will learn how to ask for what you desire. You will be guided to create your own *Manifestation Collage* and to write, think or speak a detailed plan of your desire. You will begin to open your mind and expand your thoughts to tap a higher flow of energy in preparation for *Step Three.*

STEP THREE ~ Trueprint
CONNECT WITH YOUR HIGHER SELF

A Trueprint is a map of your soul—a tool for connecting with your higher self and purpose. It's a *print* or reproduction of your *truth*. It brings forth the words, images and feelings reflective of your higher self—images and ideas that you can translate into action so that, in a very real way, you live and experience your truth, moment to moment. The more you exercise your truth, the more you build your connection to a higher level of energy, much like exercising a muscle.

Step Three will gently lead you to spend time with your own awareness and define the dynamic elements of your higher self step by step, in a language that makes sense to you, a language to which you are willing to form a commitment.

Thus, your Trueprint is very much a ritual of commitment. It becomes a personal promise to express from your higher self and create from your higher good. And it establishes an answer to the question: *What will I give myself?* It also becomes a sword to vanquish negativity—it's a very personal talisman that will sustain one-pointed thinking and ensure that all your thoughts and emotions support what you desire.

You can superimpose your Trueprint onto every event, person and object you come into contact with. It will direct you in your choices and expand what you are willing to accept, believe, expect and love in your life.

Step Three will bring you to experience the wisdom and power of a higher flow of energy such that you will soon discover yourself creating in new and innovative ways and find your life unfolding perfectly, effortlessly.

Step Four ~ Visualization

SIMULTANEOUSLY ENGAGE IN STEPS ONE, TWO AND THREE

Visualization is spending time in a concentrated, uninterrupted practise of Steps One, Two and Three together, at the same time, so that thinking more effectively becomes habitual that much quicker.

In *Step Four* you will be guided to control your thoughts, connect with the higher energy within and around you and experience your desire, in your mind's eye, as though it's actually taking place, much as you did in Steps One, Two and Three.

An increase in intuition and inspiration accompanies visualization. You needn't concern yourself with the "how" of your desire. The answers you need will be given to you. You will be guided to opportunity and will attract the surroundings and circumstances that allow for the manifestation of your desire.

Step Four is like setting aside some time to work on a project where you won't be interrupted and where you can concentrate and accomplish a great deal in only a few moments time. In fact, think of your desire as needing a certain measure of energy—say, one pound—and every thought directed toward your desire adds an ounce of energy. When you visualize, you purposefully focus all your thoughts and energy to quickly accumulate the substance of your desire.

STEP FIVE ~ Demonstration
LIVE AS THOUGH YOUR DESIRE HAS ALREADY OCCURRED

Demonstration means to act out in your life, in small, reasonable ways, the things you picture in your mind, as though they have already occurred.

Demonstration communicates to you, and to the universe, that you are truly ready to receive. It aligns your actions with your thoughts and energy. So often, we think one thing, but do another. Our actions oppose our intentions. Demonstration assembles mind, body and spirit and brings you to "be" as your higher self.

Demonstration is a simple act that greatly affects your consciousness. It will increase your imagination, forge your faith and open your mind to possibility and acceptance.

Step Five will lead you to demonstrate. For example, if you desire a mate, walk by some of the places you plan to visit with your partner. If you desire youth and vitality, you might plan a birthday party for yourself and invite a few friends over to celebrate your "sweet sixteen," no matter what your age!

It is important to start with small demonstrations and let your imagination slowly develop bigger mental concepts. You need to find reasonable ways to exercise your faith and create reality around your desire, ways that make sense to you. Doing something that seems utterly ridiculous to you will only destroy your faith, rather than enhance it.

Demonstration will place you in the path of opportunity—around people and places—where you can receive the benefits created by the energy of your thoughts, opportunities and benefits you have assured by doing this Practice.

STEP SIX ~ Manifestation

CELEBRATE THE ACHIEVEMENT OF YOUR DESIRE

Manifestation is the achievement of your desire. It is your dreams come true!

The key to remember with respect to manifestation is that what you think already exists. Manifestation is simply providing the conditions that allow for *what exists* to be made apparent to the eye.

You might think of manifestation in terms of electricity. Electricity exists even though you don't see it; what you see is the effects or manifestation of electricity, such as when you turn on a light switch and see light.

The same is true of your thoughts. The energy of your thoughts exists, though you don't immediately see it; what you see is the effects of your thoughts. The surroundings and circumstances of your life are the material representation of your mental energy.

I like to think of manifestation this way: *the check is in the mail.* When you clear your mind and focus on your desire, it exists! It's "in the mail" and on its way to you! And while you're waiting for it to arrive, you simply want to keep energy directed towards your desire to ensure that the mail isn't rerouted, lost or sent to the wrong address (in other words, dissipated, deflected or blocked by opposing or negative mental clutter.)

Step Six explores the relationship between energy and matter to give you a better understanding of how long your desire might take.

In *Step Six* you will also be guided to create a ritual of celebration for the achievement of your desires.

How to Get the Most From Your Practice

The steps are numbered to reflect a necessary order. Read and apply each step in turn. Each step reinforces the previous one, builds on what you know and prepares you for the step to come. Significantly, each step progressively increases your capacity to receive and handle a greater flow of energy. Thus, much of what you experience in later steps is the result of a shift in your energy to a higher level. If you apply later steps first, you will be somewhat like a person without taste buds enjoying a great meal—unable to fully taste your food and not even knowing what you're missing.

Know, however, that you don't have to wait until you apply all the steps to experience rewards. Each step will bring you tangible benefits, which means that you will clearly know when you have successfully assimilated a step. At this point, review and reapply the step to have it become a natural part of your day. The more you apply each step, the more profound and magical your experiences become. And the steps are intimately linked, so when you spend time engaged in one step, you automatically enhance your performance in others.

Simply, take time to enjoy your Practice. In fact, you may want to set the book down between steps. I think of this as a "parlour" book, one that is read in portions, with each portion bringing its own kind of change to your awareness, raising you to a new level of thought, emotion and action.

You will soon find yourself naturally performing all the steps in concert. And at this point, you'll know how each step works, you'll know its purpose and importance and so, like an experienced chef, you'll know just what ingredients to give more emphasis in your life, and when.

How The Practice Is Organized

The six steps are presented in six chapters. In each chapter you will find *Principles* and *Method.* The principles explain the theory behind how the Practice works. They give you a detailed look at the inner workings of thought energy. The method tells you how to put the Practice into action. It gives you the simple, practical means for using your thoughts effectively and manifesting the life you want.

The principles and method are meant to be read together, one right after the other, because effectively applying the method depends on understanding the principles, and understanding the principles is made that much easier by applying the method.

Therefore, the principles and method are broken down into small, manageable portions within each of the six steps, so that you can simultaneously explore the principles and apply the method. As you read the principles, you'll be introduced to the method and will discover how it works and why it's important. Then, as you apply the method, you'll be introduced to more detailed principles and reflection in support of your actions.

With each step you acquire a manageable portion of knowledge and immediately put it into practice in your life.

THE STEPS ARE SIMPLE

These six *simple* steps are surely that; some may say too simple. Yet, is there anything more miraculous than simplicity? These steps are small, practical, easy-to-follow steps every one of us can do. And so they should be! The power to create is natural. It's something we do every minute of the day. As we think, we continuously create.

This book simply breaks down this natural creative process into repeatable steps. Following these steps, you will become comfortable and proficient with each part of the process until you eventually find that creating the experiences and conditions you want in your life is an automatic, consistent way of being—a habit.

YOU'RE ON YOUR WAY...

Simply by reading through this material you have begun to organize your thoughts productively and elevate the energy of your thoughts and emotions. The moment you begin to implement these six simple steps, you'll find yourself performing the miracles you desire for the life of your dreams.

one-pointed thought

I saw a stagnant pool and at once removed the clutter;
within moments I saw myself in the crystal clarity and flow.

I now release all negative thoughts.
My consciousness is bathed in creativity.
All that I could ever want is right here,
where I AM.

PRINCIPLES
ATTRACTION & DIRECTION

This first set of principles describes the energy of thought so that you can develop a clear mental picture of how it works. We'll look at two principles of energy: *attraction* and *direction*. Together, these principles explain how your energy works in response to *what you think* and *how you think*. Ultimately, they explain why it is so important that you begin your Practice by taking control of both what and how you think.

By the time you finish reading through the principles of Step One, you'll be able to picture what is happening in the energy around you as you think. More importantly, though you may not see energy as yet, you will be able to clearly picture all that you are accomplishing as you take a step towards one-pointed, pure thought.

THOUGHT ENERGY

Let's begin with something familiar. Think about sound waves. And think about how sound travels from your mouth when you speak. Or think about radio waves emanating from the peak of a radio tower. In the same way, every thought sends an impulse of energy from your mind. And as you continuously think, you generate a field of energy.

At this point, we might do well to have a clearer definition of energy. When we talk about energy, we're really just talking about small particles like atoms and molecules that collect together to create a force or power. To help give this imagery, think about a time when you've looked at a ray of sun coming through a window and you could see hundreds of dust particles floating in the light.

In much the same way, the energy of your thoughts is made up of small particles inside smaller particles inside even smaller particles. These particles are so fine that they are really more like a fluid substance.

Picture the energy of your thoughts, much like water, but finer than air, flowing from your mind. The energy radiates outward in all directions, much like the rippling waves of water you see when you drop a pebble into a pool.

In fact, all things release waves of energy—people, cars, buildings, everything—which science calls matter waves. But what's really interesting is that the larger something is, the smaller its associated wave. Whereas, the smaller something is, the greater its associated wave. So, a paperclip or the book in your hands, or other more substantial physical objects, release waves of energy so small that they're hardly worth talking about. But at the subatomic level, where we are dealing with atoms and molecules and particles of energy that are really, really small, we find comparatively large waves.

Thought energy is an extremely fine and subtle form of energy that produces great waves of energy that reach out across vast distances. The energy is constantly moving and changing, creating a subtle vibration.

Thought energy vibrates at incredible speeds. To help you picture this, think about the incredibly fast movement of a hummingbird's wings. Now, imagine the wings vibrating millions of times faster. You begin to get a sense of the incredibly subtle vibration of your thoughts.

Or think about this: at best, the human ear can only hear vibrations of about forty thousand per second, a speed that is near impossible to understand. Yet, light vibrates at five hundred billion vibrations per second. And an x-ray vibrates at two trillion vibrations per second. And as if that's not mind-boggling enough, thought energy is well above any of these physical grades and types of energy!

There are, however, subtle variations in thought. Thought is energy we can control and it vibrates in varying degrees, from very high to relatively low vibrations. When our thoughts are clear and positive and we feel secure, relaxed and uplifted, the energy we generate is fine, subtle and highly vibratory. When our thoughts are negative and we feel down, unsure or uptight, the energy slows down and vibrates at a relatively slower rate.

THE PRINCIPLE OF ATTRACTION

One property of thought energy is that it *attracts* to other energy of a similar quality or vibration.

As such, when you think positively, feel good, upbeat or generally "on top of the world," you magnetize your life to similar conditions and therefore experience serendipity, luck, miracles and positive coincidences.

Conversely, when you think in a negative manner, the energy you release is vibrating at a lower level, attracting to similar energy in the people and conditions around you. You might stub your toe or bump into a door, attracting to the low vibratory nature of physical matter, or experience negative life events such as lack, hurt or limitation.

> Thought energy attracts to other energy of a similar quality or vibration.

In short, attraction tells us that positive thoughts attract to other highly vibratory energy and negative thoughts attract to their low-vibrating counterparts. So it seems that even on a subatomic level, misery loves company!

Now, let me add that *attraction* is a widely discussed and accepted effect and it's easy to understand why. We can immediately recognize the effects of attraction in our daily lives, and in so many ways. For example, when we feel good, we tend to find ourselves around others who share similar feelings and attitudes and we encounter more positive behaviors and activities. In other words, we experience what we put out into the world. This principle tells us we experience this because attraction is a fundamental effect operating at even the most basic or micro level.

However, while attraction is certainly a common-sense principle, it can also be a somewhat confusing principle, because it tells us what, but not how. It tells us that similar energy attracts, but it doesn't offer much in the way of explanation. And this can lead to confusion, because when we think of attraction and try to imagine how it works, we tend to think of magnets. And in the case of magnets, with their positive and negative poles, we know that "opposites attract." If you have ever tried to put two similarly charged magnets together, you know that it just doesn't work. So, how can we now say that similar energy *attracts?*

Add to this confusion the fact that when we're first taught about energy in school, we're introduced to the small particles of energy that inhabit and surround the nucleus of an atom: electrons, protons and neutrons. We're told that electrons, with their *negative* charge, attract to protons, with their *positive* charge; whereas, two electrons or two protons repel one another.

Clearly opposites attract! Like energy *repels* like! So, how can we now say that similar energy *attracts?*

This is a point worth addressing, because part of the purpose of our journey together is to explore these principles in detail, so we can leave behind many older questions and begin to ask new ones. Therefore, let me say this: it's easy to understand how similar energy *attracts*, we need only to return to the last example and remember that within the nucleus of an atom we find many protons, *similar* energy, tightly packed and *attracted* together. In this case, similar energy is held together by an attractive force much stronger—a hundred times stronger—than the force associated with positive and negative charges. Interestingly, science calls this strong force the "strong" force (no mystery here).

And so it is that when we talk about energy of higher levels, such as the energy of our thoughts, we are talking about a much stronger force of attraction. Tongue in cheek, we might say that the attractive force generated by the vibrations of our thoughts is the "stronger" force or the "heavy-weight" of attractive forces. Sure, thought energy has a magnetic-*like* quality. It unites energy. It forces a powerful connection. But it's not limited to attracting the opposite quality, as is the case with magnets, or even the same quality for that matter!

Thought energy produces such a strong attractive force that it exerts a powerful influence on all energy. Again, this is something we frequently experience in our daily lives. We often say "she brings me down" or "he has great vibes," because we recognize the different vibratory states of energy around us and can feel the strong influence they have on our own.

Perhaps you've had the experience of being in a room full of people where everyone is feeling somewhat "down." In walks someone whose energy is "up," and suddenly many people begin to feel a lift in their emotions. Or, you get on the bus in the morning. You're feeling fantastic, but ten minutes into the journey, you are feeling really low and can't figure out why. You look around and everyone is reading disturbing news in the paper. You are being overwhelmed by the energy around you.

The point to remember is that the energy of your thoughts is a powerful attractive force, so powerful that it not only shares an intimate connection with similar energy, it also influences the quality of all energy. Said more accurately, *thought energy of one quality or vibration tends to affect in other energy the same rate of motion.* This is an effect you can see. When you strike a piano key, vibrations are created. And if you then hold a small metal tuning fork next to the piano, the fork will immediately begin to vibrate with the same rate of motion.

Similarly, the energy you produce raises or lowers the energy around you causing it to reflect your state of mind. At the same time, you align yourself with all similar vibrations. Thus, the energy you pour into the world returns to you more of the same. Hence, the old adage, "as you sow, so shall you reap."

To help you form a mental picture of attraction, think of it as more of an attunement. Imagine it like sound. Imagine that as you think a thought, it is very much like opening your mouth and sounding out, "Ah." Now, imagine that as you do this, someone stands beside you and does the same. Now imagine that as you continue to repeat the same sound, one person after another gathers around you and intones, "Ah." More and more, the vibrations of sound will deepen within you, until you can feel your entire body resonating. So it is that as you think, you attune yourself with a chorus of similar energy.

> The energy you pour into the world returns to you more of the same.

From time to time, refresh your mind of the rich and intriguing details of *attraction*, though you can easily remember the basics of this first principle: positive thoughts produce positive events and negative thoughts produce negative events.

The Principle of Direction

Another property of energy is that it can be directed, which means that we can command energy to seek out and attract the energy of particular people and things.

Directing the energy of our thoughts is much like directing the waves of sound produced when we speak. For example, we can project our voice towards particular people and things. If we call out someone's name, we direct a more specific response. If we speak loud and clear, we project our voice farther and it's more likely to be received and understood. Whereas, if we mumble or whisper, sound barely travels.

Directing the energy of our thoughts works similarly. For example, if we think about a particular person, the energy of our thoughts immediately moves to that person, to interact and attract energy, as we command. We might think about a friend we haven't seen in years. In response to our thoughts that person might suddenly call to say, "I just had the urge to call you."

If our thoughts are clear and focused, energy is directed across a greater distance and is more likely to be understood. If we repeat a particular thought, it's more likely to be received. On the other hand, when our thoughts are fleeting or vague and unspecific, as the majority of our thoughts are, the energy isn't directed anywhere in particular, but hovers about us. If our thoughts are muddled, energy dissipates.

Of course, while we are able to direct our energy at other people, regardless of how far away they may be, in order for it to be received and understood, the other person must be relaxed and receptive. If someone is concentrating on a difficult task or fired up about their own concerns, they will absorb the incoming energy and intensify their own thoughts.

In fact, this is true in general: if our thoughts are clear and focused, we take in energy and use it for our own purposes. Consequently, we are less affected by any negative energy around us, because we simply transform it for our own use.

This is important because, as we direct energy towards others and things, we need to remember that energy is being directed towards us, sometimes purposefully, while other times, we inadvertently cross paths with the energy of others. If we keep our thoughts clear and focused, we will be better able to control the energy we experience.

What we think also has an affect on our ability to direct energy effectively. Again, this works much like sound. If we direct negative words towards others, we affect ourselves, first and foremost. We tend to isolate ourselves; we're more likely to be ignored. At best, we simply attract more of the same. The same is true when we direct negative thoughts towards another person or thing. Negative thoughts lower the vibratory rate of our energy, weakening it so that it cannot be directed effectively. As such, negative energy tends to collect around us and impact our life—a seemingly protective design of the universe.

If our negative thoughts are centered on our own concerns, problems, fears, angers or doubts, energy is directed inward. A wise woman I know calls this "self-sucking" and "self-eating." After a while, our internal nibbling so drains our energy that it takes more mental strength to achieve fewer results. Eventually, simply getting out of bed in the morning can be a monumental task.

If self-directed negative thoughts continue, we begin to use the energy from our physical sources, such as air, food and water, to fuel our mental and emotional needs. Eventually, we draw upon the energy of our cells and organs. In time, we experience physical ailments as the energy fields of our bodies are slowly drained and go through a process of entropy or slow degradation and decay.

Positive thoughts, on the other hand, have an altogether different effect on us. Positive energy, as we know from the principle of attraction,

> Energy is immediately discharged from your mind to search out and attract the conditions most similar to what you imagine.

is highly vibratory and subtler and, as such, can be directed with ease. Positive thoughts are less tiring; we use less energy. Positive thoughts insulate the body. At the same time, we attract the more abundant energy all around us, continuously supplying all systems within our body with the energy they need.

In short, you can easily remember the *principle of direction* as your ability to command energy to flow toward specific people, events and things. If you think about a specific thing or event that you want in your life, energy is immediately discharged from your mind to search out and attract the conditions most similar to what you imagine. If your thoughts are elevated and intense or clear, the energy travels a greater distance and has a greater impact. And when you repeat a particular thought, energy accumulates and creates a stronger, magnetic-like force that will quickly attract to what you hold in your mind.

What and How We Think

As you can see, *what* we think is important. What we think creates a positive or negative *attractive* force. And specific, detailed images or ideas command energy to flow in a specific *direction* and search out and attract the conditions that will bring us the things we imagine.

Which brings us to *how* we think. We don't often think about *how* we think—we simply think. Yet, how we think has an enormous impact on our ability to create. For example, a typical morning thought process might look something like this:

We wake up and think, "I have to make breakfast," which is a fairly neutral thought, one we don't feel particularly happy or unhappy about. A few minutes later, we're angry with our partner, snap at the kids and our energy slows to a lower vibratory rate. Traveling to work, we might put on headphones or switch on a radio, and we start to feel relaxed and elevate our energy as we listen to our favorite music. Then, as we arrive at work, our thoughts start flipping about like fish out of water. We start thinking about our weight, opening our own business, needing a holiday, and the energy of our thoughts is sent flying off in all directions.

Typically, our energy is up one moment, down the next. We command energy to move in one direction and moments later it's, "Wait, stop; go this way."

If our thoughts are generally positive, a few negative or distracting thoughts hardly make a difference. However, if we tend to think in a disorganized fashion, such that our mind is regularly cluttered up by opposing or negative ideas and images, we consistently interrupt, and at times completely block, the flow of energy from our mind. We short-circuit the lines of communication. When our energy is never sent in any one direction for any length of time, it attracts a hodge-podge of mixed blessings, and fails to attract or form as we desire. Additionally, we leave ourselves open to be pushed and shoved by the energy around us and often end up thinking and feeling like a yo-yo.

There is an important adage to remember as we move into Step One: our ability to create is limited not so much by our negative thoughts themselves, but by the disorganization and confusion they cause. For example, if we decide, "I want a new job," but moments later think, "I'll never find a better job," one thought effectively cancels the other.

In other words, negative (distracting, competitive) mental clutter keeps us from directing a steady stream of energy toward a desired objective, which would allow for the creation of form.

As you can see, "how" we think or organize our thoughts determines the effectiveness of "what" we think.

Bringing Thought into Form

In order to bring our thoughts into physical form, we must first become aware of *what* and *how* we think.

By reading through this information, you have taken a giant step towards creating the life you want. You can picture the powerful influence your mind has on the world around you. Which means that you now have it in your mind to be conscious of your thoughts and to notice your thought process.

Indeed, you are unique among all other creatures. You can think and think about yourself thinking! Which means that you can control the energy of your thoughts. You can connect with various levels of energy around you through the principles of attraction and direction, and mould and change the subtle substance that makes up the conditions of your life. Your consciousness—your being—is a natural creative force.

ONE-POINTED THOUGHT

We could stop right here and say, "That's it, we're ready to create." We will be aware of what occupies our mind and focus on the things we want in life!

But there's a catch—most of us carry around a few distracting, negative thoughts that hide from our conscious awareness. These are our repeating negative habits. Being unaware of these unconscious intruders, we don't control them. And what ends up happening is that, as we try to produce positive and productive energy to create what we want in life, these repeating negative habits consistently work against us.

For the most part, these negative thoughts go unchecked simply because we have become accustomed to them. They are always lurking beneath the surface of our mind, creeping in so regularly that we no longer pay attention to them. For example, it may be habit to think or say "I can't" so often that we no longer notice we do it.

Most of us have looked at another person and thought, "How can they not see this about themselves?" Nearly everyone's mind is cluttered with painful memories, fears, guilt, doubts, sadness, angers or regrets that have simply become old mental habits. These thoughts systematically clutter our mind, forming barriers and blockages that deflect the energy of our thoughts and diminish its effects.

This is why the first step toward creating your desires is to clearly identify habitually negative thoughts. The *Method* described here in Step One is a simple and effective means to do just that: clearly identify any mental clutter so that you can remove it from your path and release a steady stream of energy toward your desires. After that, manifestation will be a surprisingly simple process. By holding an image in your mind for a few minutes at a time, you will begin to manifest what you imagine.

By taking care at the start of the Practice, you will soon develop a creative *habit* of mind. You will likely use the knowledge and tools in Step One for the first two or three days until you feel your energy rising and you become aware of your more dominant negative mental clutter. But you will soon have control over your thoughts. Even your more fleeting thoughts will be fuelled with creative energy. And you will begin to manifest abundant and rewarding events with little or no conscious effort.

Step One is the first step toward controlling your thoughts and emotions and, ultimately, your destiny. It's the first step toward pure, uncluttered, one-pointed thought. Through the practise of Step One, your mind will be filled with thoughts that have a definite and dynamic purpose in the creation of your desires.

Metaphorically, each thought is a carefully selected arrow that you aim at a specific target and launch with expert control. And since no negative or contradictory thoughts clutter your mind, every thought sails unobstructed to instantly hit its target, returning the glory of its mark to you.

The *Method* that follows includes two parts: *Mental* and *Physical Clearing*. Both will expunge your life of clutter and move you toward one-pointed thinking.

Both *Methods* are simple, effective and preliminary. Combined with the additional five steps, they will essentially force you to adopt and routinely practice a positive and organized pattern of thought until you are, quite naturally and habitually, *being* happy. More importantly, you are automatically releasing bountiful and rewarding energy that will attract the best possible circumstances in any given moment. If you did little else, this clear and focused pattern of thought alone would lead you to your best life.

METHOD I

MENTAL CLEARING

FROM GARBAGE TO GURU:
SORTING THROUGH YOUR THOUGHTS

As a first step toward creating your desires, you must first empty out the contents of your mind—you need to see what's there! You can then clearly and deliberately sort through your thoughts and identify what's treasure and what's clutter. Next, you can reorganize your thinking, keeping only the treasure. You will now have the awareness to make and keep a commitment to never again allow mental clutter to "mess up" your mind, disrupting the neat, tidy, and focused organization of your thoughts.

INVENTORY JOURNALING

This first Method will take you through the creation of your own Inventory Journal—a quick and effective means to examine your thoughts and discharge negative mental clutter.

The word "inventory" describes the act of making a complete and detailed list of your traits. "Journaling" refers to the act of moving thoughts from your mind to a piece of paper or recording device, without editing.

Inventory Journaling is the act of making a clear and detailed list of your negative and limiting beliefs without dwelling on them. It's a structured form of journaling—a small step. And it will quickly provide you with a physical representation of the clarity or clutter of your thoughts.

Before we begin, let's quickly review what constitutes a "negative" thought. And, let's understand what it means to say that we don't want to "dwell" on these thoughts.

WHAT IS A NEGATIVE THOUGHT?

For our purposes, the word "negative" refers to any thought that pulls your mind away from a positive and productive focus—your desires and the things you want in your life.

For example, someone might say, "when I get more time, I'll do this or that." Now, this thought doesn't seem particularly negative, but if it keeps you from focusing on the things you want in your life, then it is having the same effect as if you had thought, "I'm afraid to do this or that right now," or "I can't do this or that right now." However a thought is expressed, if it isn't helping you, then it is a negative or disruptive thought—clutter.

DUMP DON'T DWELL

Dealing with our negative clutter doesn't have to be a painful experience. In fact, suffering over it only makes things worse and defeats the purpose. The key throughout this exercise is to *dump out* your negative thoughts instead of dwelling on them. Dwelling on pain only gives it more energy.

Think about it this way: our thoughts are living entities that we can choose to either feed or starve. Remember, every thought is an impulse of energy that immediately starts to shape and mould the external conditions of your life. The more you concentrate on pain or fear, the more you lower your energy, which in turn attracts more of the same into your life.

As you create your journal, if you find yourself suddenly caught up or stuck, dwelling on particular pains, with your mind going around and around in circles, consider some of the following points.

We often dwell on certain negative thoughts or events because we get caught up in the details, such as what we lost, how much it hurts or what somebody said to us. When this happens, we move farther and farther away from simply accepting the thought and dumping it. For example, we might say, "I don't understand why Joanne is always so mean. Joanne makes me so angry." Instead of focusing on Joanne it's much more effective to simply say, "You know what? I'm angry. That's the bottom line. I'm the one who's angry here, and I can do something about that."

> Every thought is an impulse of energy that immediately starts to shape and mould the external conditions of your life.

Until we clearly identify our negative thoughts, we remain far away from removing them, and the details continue going around and around in our minds.

Sometimes we dwell on our negative thoughts because we want to figure out where they came from: "How did this anger or upset get into my mind? Why am I so afraid of what will happen next week?"

If we do figure out how a particular pain or fear got into our mind, quite often it still doesn't change the fact that it's there. If, for example, we discover that a childhood experience brought about the fear we have now, this discovery itself doesn't suddenly whisk away our fear. It may only change how we approach the solution or what method we choose to overcome our fear. But, no matter what solution we choose, we will need to practice a new way of thinking in order to establish a new way of behaving in order to form a new habit. To choose a new way of thinking, we have to clearly identify our negative thoughts.

Finally, if we continually dwell on certain negative thoughts then it's worth considering that we might be wanting to fuel our anger or pain rather than letting them go. Crazy as it sounds, it can be hard to move away from what's familiar; even when it hurts it becomes comfortable.

In short, we sometimes spend considerable time on introspection and analysis as a way to avoid moving forward. As long as we're digging up the dirt, there's no reason to start planting. It's easy to fear change. And we don't always have a good reason to let go. But now you do. Identifying your negative thoughts will allow you to carry out a few very simple steps so you can perform miracles in your life.

Go ahead and dig up all the barriers to your creative power, but know that you don't have to spend time dwelling on them. In other words, turn over the dirt in your mind, but know that you don't have to play in it. If it feels good or comfortable to explore certain thoughts and feelings, do so. But don't feel that you have to. Simply create a clear and detailed inventory of your negative thoughts.

You will find that by taking a few small steps, you can quickly and effectively dissolve the barriers to your creative power.

CREATING YOUR INVENTORY JOURNAL

Inventory Journaling has three distinct stages:
• Prompts
• Fears
• Jailers

"Prompts" assist you to continuously write (or speak, if you are using a recorder). This is what is traditionally known as journaling. It can induce a trance-like state that allows some of your more unconscious thoughts to surface.

"Fears" involves consciously sorting through your mental clutter. To use an analogy, the "prompts" section is like going into the attic to find the boxes stored away. The "Fears" section is opening up the boxes to see what's hiding inside.

"Jailers" is taking inventory of the clutter and naming what is holding you back.

PROMPTS

To begin, find a quiet place where you won't be disturbed. For your first time through this exercise, set aside thirty minutes or a bit longer. After this, you may only need a few minutes a day to jot down additional points, when they come up.

You will need a pen and paper or a recording device to speak into. (You may also ask someone to assist you if this feels more comfortable for you.)

Below are twelve numbered prompts, simple phrases designed to stimulate your thoughts. They represent some of the more common ways in which our negative and distracting thoughts are expressed.

Read each prompt, keeping in mind the different areas of your life, and list the first few thoughts that come to mind, if any. If nothing comes to mind, move on to the next prompt.

For example:

"I worry…"

Make a list of any worries and anxieties that come into your mind. Don't second-guess your thoughts. Don't edit out any expression about an event, object or person. If a thought comes to mind, write it down, even if it seems silly or stupid. It should feel like you are spewing out the clutter in your mind.

You might write:

"I worry about not having enough money."
"I worry I'll lose my job."
"I worry about what other people think."
"I worry that as soon as something good happens, something bad will happen."

Don't "worry" about expressing yourself logically. Simply keep moving through the numbered prompts and allow the contents of your mind to flow out onto paper or into a recorder.

Keep in mind that, as you record a few things under one heading, you might suddenly think of something else you would like to add to a previous section. The order in which you write doesn't matter. You may write down a thought in response to Prompt #1 (I worry…) and later as you read Prompt #5 (I can't…), you recall another worry. Just go ahead and write down your worry under heading #5. You simply want to spill out any negative thoughts, in any order, as they come to mind.

The important thing is that you write down, or in some way record, your mental clutter. You want to see or hear your thoughts outside of you and make them into something tangible. You want a clear recording of your dominant negative thoughts so you can later replace them with the tools in the Practice.

Go ahead now and work your way through the prompts. Remember, don't spend too long on any one prompt. If you find that nothing comes to mind for one or several of the prompts, that's fine, skip them and move on. These prompts are simply intended to jog your memory and stimulate your thoughts.

Examples of possible responses follow each prompt.

TWELVE PROMPTS

1. **"I worry…"**

   "I worry that I've tried so hard before and nothing seems to work. What if I try again and it doesn't work, or I hate it?"

   "I worry about my health."

2. **"I fear…"** or **"I'm afraid…"**

   "I fear I don't have enough knowledge to do what I want."

   "I fear time is running out and I'm just getting older and not accomplishing anything."

"I'm afraid to do what I want—what if it all falls apart, what will everyone say?"

3. **"I feel guilty..."**

"I feel guilty that I didn't help Tom on Saturday."

"I feel guilty that I haven't made more of an effort to see my mother."

"I feel guilty that I procrastinate."

4. **"I don't have control..." "I have no control over..."**

"I don't have control over my life. There's too much to do and never any time for me."

"I have no control over others."

"It doesn't seem to matter what I do, I have no control over what life hands me."

5. **"I can't..."**

"I can't just quit my job."

"I can't follow my heart, because I don't know what my heart is telling me."

"I can't really believe I deserve anything better."

6. **"I doubt..." "I don't believe..."**

"I doubt everyone can have everything."

"I don't believe it's possible for me, it's just that simple."

"I don't believe I can do this."

7. **"There's never enough time..."**

"There's never time to do what I want to do."

"There isn't time to start something new."

"I never seem to get a long enough break to feel truly rested."

8. **"I find it hard to forgive…"**

"How can I possibly forgive Ray? Not for what he's done. No way."

"I find it hard to forgive myself. There are things about me that I don't like."

"How can I forgive? I lost so much—too much—I'll never get that time back."

9. **"What I don't want to do anymore is…" "I don't want…"**

"What I don't want to do anymore is work. I've had enough. I want a break."

"I don't want pain anymore."

"I don't want to keep attracting people who hurt me instead of helping me."

10. **"What really hurts is…"**

"What really hurts is how much I do for other people, and when I need something, no one is around."

"My joints hurt, I hate this more than anything."

"What really hurts is how hard I try and people always have something negative to say about me."

11. **"I feel …"**

"I feel bad and I hate it. I just don't know how to turn it around."

"I feel frustrated. When will I have loved enough, tried enough, been good enough, when? When is it my turn?"

"I'm always second-guessing myself or my decisions, worried about what people think."

12. **"I regret…"**

"I regret not doing more of what I want to do. I always try and do the right thing. I worry about the future. I don't want to disappoint anyone."

"I regret not letting things go. I replay things in my mind for days."

FEARS

As a next step in creating your Inventory, go back over the statements you made for #1 and #3 to #12 (You can skip #2: "I fear…") and see if you can identify a fear in any of the negative thoughts you listed. Ask yourself, "What could I possibly be afraid of in this anger, worry, guilt, doubt or negative expression?"

You don't need to spend a lot of time wracking your brain to find an answer, but try this as a challenge and see if you can uncover a hidden fear. Here are some examples of how fear might be discovered beneath other emotions.

"I worry about what others think" might be connected to several fears:

"I'm afraid other people won't like me."

"I'm afraid there's something wrong with me."

"I'm afraid I won't get ahead."

"I'm different from other people. I've always felt this. Maybe deep down I worry that there's a part of me that is damaged or isn't as good as others. I worry about what others think because I'm afraid they'll see the part of me that I believe is ugly."

"*I find it hard to forgive* Tom, and I'm angry" might be connected to:

"I'm afraid that I'm actually like Tom. I've made similar mistakes. I do the same things sometimes. There is a part of me I don't like and it's the part that is just like Tom."

"I'm afraid that Tom is the winner and I'm the loser."

"I fear that I'm weak. I let Tom and others push me around. Instead of standing up for what I believe or just walking away, I take it. I let myself get drawn into an argument and I end up angry. I'm really angry at myself, because I let fear keep me from speaking up or walking away from abuse."

"*I feel* jealous and envious of Rhonda" might be connected to:

"I'm afraid I'll never have what I want."

"I'm afraid I'll always be less and others will always have more."

"I'm angry at the world, because deep down, I'm afraid that some people get and others don't and I'm one of the 'don'ts'."

"Things always work out for Rhonda. Maybe there really is something wrong with me."

"*I feel* angry at my parents" might be connected to:

"I haven't really treated my parents the way I would like to do. I fear I never will."

"I'm afraid of being alone."

"I'm afraid I'll be like them."

"I carry a lot of pain from how my parents treated me. I hate this. I fear that somehow I'm damaged and I'll never be happy because of it. I'm afraid I missed out. I'm afraid I can't let it all go and I will waste the rest of my life carrying this pain around."

Rephrasing negative/distracting statements as fears is often the best way to clearly identify a deeply planted seed of negativity.

For example, in rephrasing the statement, "I'm angry at my parents," I wrote, "I'm afraid I missed out. I fear I'm damaged." To me, this speaks to how I see myself and clearly reveals that, deep down, I don't feel completely okay with me. And so, I added to my Inventory Journal: I need to look at how I love myself.

By rewriting my statement of anger as a fear, I identified a deeply rooted seed of negativity. Now I can stop wasting energy on anger and address a fundamental blockage continually draining my energy.

Keep in mind that the word "fear" has taken on an ugly connotation for most of us. It tends to be equated with weakness. And so, most of us would rather admit to being anything other than fearful.

But fear is simply our natural human response to distress. It's a key part of our "fight or flight" response. This means that when something is distressing, our natural impulse is to protect ourselves by either fighting or fleeing. For example, if someone upsets you, you either want to "punch their lights out" or hide and cringe.

Every negative thought has a seed of fear at its core. This fear is simply a natural response to a negative event and may appear in the form of anger or the need to get away and withdraw in some manner.

You may find it difficult to rephrase some statements as a fear. Try it as a challenge, it can be well worth it. You may just discover a key bit of clutter that, once removed, opens the floodgates, releasing a powerful stream of energy. For example, I held anger towards someone for years. When I tried to rethink my anger in terms of "fear," I kept thinking, "no, I'm just really, really angry." But I was curious, so I thought about it for a few days. Eventually, I realized I was angry at how this person treated me because I was afraid that I often treat myself in the same way and would likely do so again! As it turned out, identifying this single bit of clutter was one of the most useful things I've done for myself.

Rephrasing negative/distracting statements as fears is also a way of bringing your concerns home, acknowledging your negative thoughts and their roots as your own, accepting and taking responsibility for them. We need to own our negative habits if we are going to get rid of them. Said another way, it's a lot easier to take out our own garbage.

For example, we might say, "I'm angry at my parents." This statement projects our emotions away from us. It suggests that our parents have responsibility for our emotions or that we require them to do or say something before we can deal with our emotions. As long as we stay focused on the parents, we leave our garbage on their doorstep, not our own.

But if we rephrase our anger as a fear and say, "Actually, I'm afraid of doing everything on my own" or "I'm afraid I don't have someone to love me," we take possession of our thoughts and clearly identify the doubt or anxiety that's eating at us and cluttering our mind. And now that our negative thoughts are in our possession, we can make a choice about whether or not to keep them. And this is why I say it's easier to take out our own garbage. If we leave it on someone else's doorstep, there might be too much distance between the garbage and us, and it might sit there rotting.

Jailers

At this point, you can use your journal to identify dominant themes, key words and phrases that are repeatedly expressed. These are your mental *jailers*—thoughts that are keeping you a prisoner of your own mind, just as surely as if you were physically locked away. These thoughts pull you away from focusing on the positive things you want in life. They limit your imagination and determine what you are willing to believe and accept for yourself.

Would you hire a guard to follow you around all day and grab hold of you and lock you up whenever you wanted to try something new or create something better? Probably not, and yet this is exactly the kind of power we give to our negative thoughts.

Mental clutter not only hurts and distracts us, it also deflects, dissipates and drains our flow of energy, such that we can end up feeling like a ball bearing in a pinball machine, knocked about by the energy around us.

Go back over your journal and take inventory of your prominent negative thoughts. List them as Jailer #1, Jailer #2, Jailer #3, and so on. You'll likely find that there are really only a few negative thoughts cluttering your mind—maybe even only one—but they are expressed in many different ways.

For example, looking over my answers, one dominant worry sticks out like a sore thumb: "I worry about what other people think." In several different ways and under a number of different headings, I repeated this thought, or one similar. I recorded this as:

JAILER #1: "I fear others won't like me—'people pleaser.'"

I also noticed that I was repeatedly anxious and uneasy about things and continually framed the circumstances in my life as a worry. Therefore, I added to my list:

JAILER #2: "Worry Wart."

I also included the following:

JAILER #3: "I can't."
JAILER #4: "I fear I'm not good enough—'damaged goods.'"

You can express the dominant negative themes in your life in any manner that makes sense to you. While some of your more dominant negative thoughts will be expressed as entire sentences, others may be neatly rolled into a couple of words, such as my Jailer #3, "I can't."

An example of this brevity is in Victoria's experience with Inventory Journaling. Victoria repeatedly worried about her future. She worried that she wouldn't have enough money and would end up eating cat food. Her every choice was based on what would provide her with future security—like it or not! So she summarized her concerns as "cat food," playing on the fear that she could end up so poor she'd have to eat cat food. From then on, whenever she caught herself feeling anxious she would think, "cat food," and put herself in the position to examine her thoughts and decide whether or not she was simply repeating an old negative habit that would inevitably hinder and not help her.

Complete your list of mental *jailers* by writing any word or phrase that you feel best expresses your dominant negative thoughts. Be creative. Consider the feelings and images your mental jailers evoke. You can focus on summarizing the negative—or you can create a jailer that captures the positive outcome you want.

For example, Marial wanted to do the things she loved, but they were unfamiliar and new and didn't come with a "safety net," as she expressed it. Marial was afraid to let go of the old, familiar things she felt provided her with security, so she imagined herself as a trapeze artist, someone who must let go if they are to perform successfully, and these became her code words to release her from her jailer of insecurity. Now, whenever Marial feels insecure or hesitant, she thinks, "trapeze artist," and puts herself in the position to "let go" of her fearful thoughts.

Once you complete your list, you will realize how powerful it is. In fact, seeing your negative thoughts written down or expressed outside of you is magical in its effectiveness. It's like having someone repeat your thoughts back to you, putting you in a position to look at your thoughts with detachment.

When you write out your mental clutter, it can no longer hide from you. After a time, you begin to see all the deep meanings you have attached to certain things. You begin to see that your *jailers* are really just words, events or objects—just ink on paper or a breath of air.

You will notice what negative thoughts you tend to regurgitate throughout the day, and when. Eventually, when you have repeatedly identified and acknowledged the same negative thoughts over and over, you will see these thoughts for what they are—waste.

When you repeatedly identify and acknowledge the same negative thoughts over and over, you will see these thoughts for what they are—waste.

PUTTING YOUR INVENTORY INTO PRACTICE

You now have a clear and definitive list of *jailers*, key words and phrases that will remind you throughout the day to notice your thinking process. Carry this list with you for the first few days or weeks of your Practice. Record your *jailers* on a card that you can stick in your wallet or pocket, or jot them down in a small notebook you see regularly.

If at any time you start to feel unhappy, down, confused, worried, anxious or unsure of yourself, immediately imagine that you hear sirens. Stop and police your thoughts. Ask for identification. See if you are regurgitating any old negative habits. If you are, state them out loud, "Right, I'm just worried about what others think again!" "Okay, this is my 'I'm less' voice" or "I know you, you're my 'cat food' concern."

Remember, we want to be aware of our thoughts and keep them focused on positive and productive images and ideas to release a steady, directed stream of energy that will build our ideas into form. And if we do so for a time, it soon becomes a habit to think more deliberately, positively and pro- | Happiness is a habit. ductively. Happiness is a habit.

Said another way, positive thinking doesn't work because we rarely believe the positive thoughts we're stating. We're trying, often somewhat desperately, to convince ourselves that we're *not* something. All of which adds up to focusing on the problem. We're saying, "I'm wonderful," but thinking, "Yeah, right." Instead, productive thinking does work. When we consistently identify negative thoughts and replace them with productive thoughts—thoughts we accept and believe, thoughts of things we want and enjoy—it soon becomes a habit to think productively, focusing more and more on the people, events and things that benefit our life.

If you discover yourself expressing a new negative or distracting thought, write it down and add it to your list. You want to learn to recognize rambling, negative and crippling thoughts so you can thank them for stopping by, shake their hand and let them go, replacing them with any of the exercises and creative thoughts from Steps Two, Three, Four, Five and Six.

Remember, it's easy to be ruled by our negative thoughts and beliefs. But the worst of it is that we're not always aware that we're releasing negativity into our life and limiting our ability to create. And then we're left to wonder why things are not working out!

You've taken an incredible step toward using the laws of energy and creating everything you want in your life quickly and easily. You have brought into your awareness what and how you think, and you now have the means to identify the dominant mental clutter that repeats in your thoughts and disrupts your energy.

As you move through the Practice, you will gain a number of tools that will help you to replace your negative thoughts with creative ones. Do what you can. You don't have to try and be superhuman. Simply make the effort to be aware and let go of chaotic, negative and unproductive thoughts each time you recognize them. Every effort allows more energy to accumulate, bringing you the things you want.

A Ritual of Commitment ~ Baggage

After you complete your one clear list of *jailers*, take the notes or recordings you made in creating your Inventory Journal and cut up the paper or bust up the recordings and put the pieces into a small bag or hankie and tie it with string.

This is an important ritual. Keep this "baggage" for a while—beside your bed, on your desk at work, in your briefcase or carried with you. Let it serve as a visible reminder of the waste that comes from living in the past. Let it remind you not to put this clutter back into your thoughts. And think about how the contents of this small bag are enough to disrupt, if not block, your ability to attract and direct energy and manifest your dreams.

Make a commitment to work with your *jailers* and keep this bag for thirty days and then, simply burn it.

The Joy of Negativity ~ Congratulate Yourself!

At this point, take a moment and congratulate yourself for every negative thought you own. Yes, congratulate yourself. If you can choose negativity then this means that you also have the power to choose positivity! Your negative thoughts don't have power—you have power!

Spend a quiet, serious moment congratulating yourself and thanking your pain, anger and fears. They have developed you. If you can cope every day with upset and heartache, then you have forged incredible will power. You have developed amazing strength and powers of concentration and imagination. You have a remarkable set of creative skills with which to manifest your dreams.

Remember, every day is election day. Every day we can choose to put our negative thoughts onto a throne and give them the power to rule our kingdom, or not. And if you have chosen to live with negative thoughts before, if you have lived with tyrants every day of your life, imagine the release you'll experience in living with freedom!

Imagine what you can do by giving all your power to creative thoughts instead of negative ones.

A Review of Mental Clearing

Our ability to create on command depends on upon our ability to think clearly and positively. It's important, therefore, to bring into our awareness the dominant mental clutter that threatens this ability.

"Take inventory and take control!"

Inventory Journaling is a small, simple step. While it can take as little as a few minutes a day, it's very effective. Simply record the negative thoughts that circulate in your mind and make a clear list of recurring or dominant themes. This will help you become aware of your thoughts and release hidden concerns. It will assist you in quickly recognizing when your thinking is being dominated by repeating negative habits. Ultimately, this will allow more creative energy to flow in and replace the clutter.

I've spoken to a number of people who tell me that they have spent considerable time journaling in the past and wonder if they might skip this first Method. I recommend taking at least a few minutes at the start of this Practice to create a clear list of your more dominant negative thoughts, even if you have previously done journaling, as this is journaling with a very specific purpose.

It's best to take as much time as you need at the start of the Practice to "let it all out." At some point, you will feel that there are no old negative thoughts left to express. You may still feel angry, hurt or doubtful, but you will feel that you have listed and identified your main concerns, which is the first step to removing them.

You may wish to come back to this exercise when you feel the need to dump residual pain or when distracting thoughts crop up along the way. It is often not until you progress through the Practice that some of your more deeply hidden fears and obstructions start to rise up from the depths.

Over the next few days or more, write or record any new negative thoughts that come to mind. If you feel that you are regularly noticing when distressing thoughts enter your mind, then you have successfully taken a first step towards one-pointed thinking. You are now in a position to recognize when aimless thoughts are threatening to overtake the precise, organized thoughts of your desires.

The following are some pointers to assist you in applying Method I:

• To concentrate the creative power of your mind, take five minutes upon waking to write down the first few thoughts that come into your mind. Do the same for those thoughts circulating in your mind just before you set your head on the pillow each night.

This will help you become cognizant of your mental thought patterns. Is your manner of thought consistently organized around positive emotions and desires, or are your thoughts constantly seesawing from constructive ideas to debilitating ones?

A habitually negative perception eventually forms a "diseased perception," where it simply becomes automatic to see and respond to the world negatively. Having morning and evening check-ins can guard against this.

• You might also spend a few minutes to specifically go back over your day and try to recall every instance where you thought negatively about an event or person. Did you recognize your negative thoughts at the time?

We may in fact choose to let ourselves be angry or sad at times, but it is important that we recognize that this is our choice.

• If you identify any negative thoughts that consistently crop up and you feel that you can't move past them, then you may want to explore them a bit. If it feels comfortable, ask yourself, "Why do I need this thought? Why do I cherish it and exercise it so often?"

Think about this: if you found a bit of garbage in your home, would you cherish it? Keep it? Put it on prominent display? Of course not, and yet we do this with our negative thoughts all the time. We collect them, give them a prominent focus and look at them again and again.

• Keep in mind that, whatever you believe most deeply, you will find evidence for. If you believe you can't, you will find reason after reason to prove this to be true. If you worry, you will find proof and evidence to show that it's a legitimate worry, a reasonable, practical concern. And this can make it difficult to give up many negative thoughts. So here again, ask yourself this: *Is my negative thought, with all its proof and evidence, doing anything for me?*

A friend of mine, a police detective, believed that the world was a terrible place. And no wonder—every day he sees some pretty horrible things. But one day, I asked him, "What good does it do for you or anyone to believe that the world is a horrible place?" After a pause, he said that thinking this way made him cautious.

Then I asked, "Cautious of what?"

"Well, I have to watch my back."

"Sure, you need to be aware that there are some people and things that can harm you and others. And you are cautious because you want to keep yourself and others, even the 'bad' guys and gals, safe. That's a positive, productive, loving thought. What do you think of this thought?"

"Yeah, you could look at it that way."

"That's my point. You can look at anything any way you want. So why not take the time to ask yourself, '*What is this thought doing for me?*' And think about your answer. If it doesn't fill you with positive energy and keep you focused on things you love and want to experience, consider acknowledging the thought, writing it down and replacing it the next time it threatens to take over your thoughts."

A Metaphor ~ The Garden of Eden and the Tiger

I want to give you a metaphor to appreciate the gift you've given yourself in identifying your mental clutter—the fears that disrupt your flow of energy.

Imagine you see the most remarkable garden, your Garden of Eden. It's everything you've ever dreamed of, and in it is everything you could ever want.

But, in the next moment, a ferocious tiger appears and, all at once, the garden seems like a dream, while the tiger is ever so real. You can hear it breathing. You can smell it. You can see the saliva dripping from its teeth.

Then, just as suddenly, you cock your head and pull back a little. You have seen this tiger before—in your imagination. It is an image you created from negativity, limitation and ferocious disbelief. In this moment of recognition, you realize that you possess the most awesome power—choice.

You remain, for a time, shaken by the realism of the tiger, but eventually, you clench your hands, screw up your face and raise your foot to take one small step forward. Before your foot even touches the ground, the tiger vanishes. It was only ever made up of intention, belief and expectation. And now you intend something different, believe in something more and expect better.

As your foot touches the ground, all around you appears the most glorious garden. You smile and open your arms and eyes as wide as you can, reaching for others, wanting to share the realization that you have always been standing, just right here, in your Garden of Eden.

METHOD II
PHYSICAL CLEARING

Waste Not, Want Not

"Waste not, want not." This generally means that if you don't waste anything or throw anything away, then you'll never need anything. But it's more apt to say that if you keep an abundance of matter in your life, then it's *futile* to want anything. If you desire something, then you have to make room for it, mentally and physically.

The next act of clearing is to cleanse your life of physical clutter and make room for the guru within. Clearing should be repeated periodically. Here are some effects clearing will have on your Practice and your life.

1. CLEARING FREES UP ENERGY. You have access to an unlimited amount of energy with which to create anything you desire. But if your space is already cluttered with so much manifested energy—things— there simply isn't room to bring in something new. On the physical level, there can only be *so much* manifested energy in your environment.

Think of it this way: your environment is like a sandy beach with miles and miles of sand to shape into all sorts of things. Imagine, however, that a crowd of people suddenly swarms this sandy beach and sets up camp. The beach is now cluttered with chairs, umbrellas and coolers and you can hardly see the sand anymore. You still have the same amount of sand to work with, but you no longer have the space to create.

If you attempt to bring something new into an already cluttered environment, you may find yourself struggling to create or taking considerable time to manifest your desires.

And, at times, you may find that existing matter is falling away or leaving your life to make room for the things you want. In practical terms, this means that people in your life may come and go, friends may move away, you might be given the smaller office at work or get less of what you want or something might break down so you are forced to discard it. The purpose of all this is to free up more energy.

Simply put, clearing is, "out with the old, in with the new." As you free up space in your environment, energy always rushes right back into your life as something new and better.

For example, Emma was clearing out her kitchen. There were a few items she was reluctant to part with, such as an old cutting board that had once been burned on a stove, a set of knives and a pot. All in all, there were about five items she wanted to keep, but they were in poor shape and needed to go. Emma finally parted with all the items, all the while focusing on replacing them with new ones.

Within three days, every item came back into her life, brand new. A neighbor gave her a beautiful new chopping block. A friend gave her a new set of knives. She received an expensive phone and stereo as a gift. And, driving home one night, she spotted a garage sale where she found a set of cooking pots still in their box, offered to her for free, as the seller wanted to finish up for the day.

2. CLEARING RAISES YOUR ENERGY. This is important because, as you know, you attract to similar energy.

When you are first learning to experience yourself as a creative force, it can seem difficult to elevate your energy or to know what this feels like. When you edit much of the physical matter from your environment, you will immediately feel an energized sensation—the same sensation you want to have as you think and create.

We often experience this energizing effect when we step outside of our office, walk out onto a balcony or stand in the middle of an open field. The abundant free flow of energy immediately elevates our thoughts and energy.

You may experience the rise in your energy as a positive jolt or sense of passion or excitement. You may describe it as feeling "free" or "up." Each of us will describe this experience differently, but it is the first part of a total sensation of knowing our thoughts are creative and feeling with absolute certainty that every thought is impacting the energy around us.

Once you experience your energy in an elevated state and come to know this sensation, you can't un-know it. You will become able to recreate this experience more and more easily, at any time. And in this elevated state, nothing will interfere with your ability to create.

Initially, however, you will want to do all you can to induce this experience quickly and certainly. By editing much of the physical matter around you, which can interfere with your energy in much the same way that a cell phone can interfere with other electronic equipment, you quickly jump-start your energy and kick it into high gear.

3. CLEARING PROVES TO YOU THAT YOU CAN CHANGE. It is a concrete, physical act that establishes your commitment to moving forward.

So much of what we think is tied to our physical actions. We often say, "Don't say you're sorry, show me" or "How do I know until I see it?"

As you physically remove items from your environment, you are actively demonstrating to yourself that you are able to let go of the past, exercise confidence in the future and prepare for your creations. Seeing yourself do this, you clearly establish in your mind not only that you believe in your ability to create, but that you are willing to accept something more and expect better. You are ready to go, ready to change.

This ritual act is important, because at this stage in the Practice, while you might know that you can create, you may well experience this more as an abstract concept of what is possible and *right*. Clearing brings you closer to experiencing your ability as *true*.

4. CLEARING INCREASES YOUR CAPACITY FOR ENERGY. In truth, you have an unlimited capacity for energy, but if your mind and environment are full of clutter, this capacity is diminished.

As with one-pointed thought, clearing prepares you to accept and handle a greater flow of energy, because it elevates your energy and opens up your mind and expands your thinking. Clearing also instantly gives you this greater flow, because it invites and attracts an influx of energy into your life.

Clearing helps you live as a greater vessel for energy, so that you can receive, retain, generate and direct more energy toward your desires.

CLEARING

Go through your living space—your room, home, closets, drawers, cupboards, car, garage, office, purse—and, as much as possible, remove everything that is not immediately useful. Strip away all the clutter and keep only what is essential for day-to-day living. If there are legal or accounting papers you require, organize them and label them as you go. Everything should have a purpose and a place.

This simple act will give you an immediate experience of what would otherwise take years to achieve. You will feel freer, as though a weight has been removed that had been compressing your breathing. You will feel your energy rise and your mind become clearer.

REMEMBER CLARA'S STORY...

You'll remember that Clara had very little. She lived in a sparsely furnished bachelor suite. However, although Clara can now well afford to live an opulent lifestyle, she instead keeps her living space organized according to functionality. Each object serves a purpose. She requires renewal and so there is a bed for this purpose. She requires love and so there are minimalist furnishings for the purpose of communion with others. She requires nourishment and so the kitchen is organized to supply exactly what she needs to drink, heat soup, make toast, serve and eat.

Her environment is a reflection of the uncluttered, organized functionality of her thoughts. Every thought revolves around clear goals and has a clear purpose to aid in the creation of her desire. Her emotions support the anticipated end result. There is no clutter. Indeed, she simply cannot comprehend any emotion or thought in contradiction to her goal. Consequently, she creates more of what she desires and creates it faster.

> Clearing will help you become a greater vessel for energy, able to receive, retain, generate and direct more energy toward your desires.

This is what we want to achieve. We want our thoughts and environment to be reflections of one another, reflections of clarity.

Look around you and take inventory of all the things that never get looked at or used. Notice the various objects you profess an attachment towards. Take note of all the memories you've lugged around from place to place that are now overflowing in cupboards and drawers. The various attachments we've collected physically are often indicative of how much we allow our thoughts to resonate with past thinking.

There is nothing wrong with collectibles or sentiment, but being attached to the things themselves, rather than honoring the energy or memories they carry, can weigh you down. Life is infinite, physical objects are not. Things do not go with you through life, but your energy, in the form of your experiences and feelings, does.

Realize that sentiment is feelings and mental attitude. And your feelings and attitudes are the mental juices that fuel your creative energy. Sentiment is wonderful, but it should live in your heart, not in things. Rather than looking at things to re-live the past and reminisce, honor your memories and experiences by giving them life. Let them live in your thoughts, emotions and actions. Express them in how you interact with yourself and others. Sentiment is an attitude, not a thing.

Simply, things have a way of tethering our creativity. There is little reason to think creatively when our minds are constantly stimulated by an abundance of clutter or sentiment that chains us to things.

Keep in mind also that many of the items we cling to from our past can build a sense of complacency. We wrap ourselves in familiar things to feel safe. We surround ourselves with more and equate this with *being* more. And after a while, our environment can feel like a warm, cozy bed we don't want to leave. Indeed, we can even begin to fear leaving it. And so, we hope for more, but deep down we're not ready for change. Instead, we need to recognize that we are strong, powerful and secure and let go of all that holds us back.

When we keep the same external influences in our lives, we are often moved to carry out the same old course of thought and, therefore, emotions and actions. Often, this means that we spend our time ruminating on the past or anticipating the future. Instead, we want to establish a present-oriented, organized, positive and creative pattern of thought.

By eliminating old, distracting and emotionally demanding stimuli from your physical surroundings, you greatly enhance your ability to think in new and innovative ways. You enhance your ability to think clearly. And you increase your ability to control your thoughts and emotions and focus on the present.

THINK SIMPLICITY & FUNCTIONALITY

As much as possible, try to limit everything in your surroundings to your current needs. Think simplicity and functionality.

Leave as much empty space as you can in whatever area you are clearing: your home, car and work space. The goal is to be able to mentally review your living space and be able to recall everything stored on shelves, in cupboards, drawers and closets. You don't need to be able to list the title of every book on a bookshelf or say how many bars of soap are stored in a cupboard under the sink, but you should know what and where everything is in your living space. If there is a trunk or drawer somewhere and you're not sure what's tucked away inside, go through it.

Collectibles & Memories

You may find it difficult to remove many collectibles and memories. You don't need to throw them away, but carefully consider the usefulness and importance of each item and, perhaps, package some items for storage. You might keep one shelf for collectibles instead of several and you could rotate your keepsakes in and out of storage for interest and inspiration.

If you find that you haven't missed anything or needed any of the items you placed in storage, in six months time tell a friend where to find your boxes and ask him or her to discard everything. If you go yourself, you might be tempted to cart it all home again. If you feel it might be worth it, ask your friend to hold a sale and give the proceeds to charity.

A Personal Illustration

I found the act of clearing my physical surroundings to be one of the single most liberating acts of my life. To assist myself, I made a deal with a friend. We swapped apartments for the weekend with the intent of discarding anything not having the immediate purpose of sustaining life. For my part, I left my friend with one directive: the chairs in the corner of my living room were not mine and could not be disposed of.

I arrived home on the Sunday night to twenty large garbage bags lined up along the wall in the hallway. I have no idea what was inside the twenty bags or how a tiny one-bedroom suite could even hold such an amount of goods, or "bads," as the case may be. My friend did confess that a great majority of the bags contained some interesting frozen food stuffs that had taken some time to discard.

I wasn't sure I could go through with it and I begged for a moment to look inside the bags. In the end, I settled for a walk through the apartment. I could not identify anything missing, but the cupboards were bare except for the most immediate of necessities. Even my clothes had been sorted of 'holy' remnants. Everything hung neatly in place and my drawers and closets looked like store displays.

With this single ritual, I resolved to never again allow clutter to occupy my life. And as my life is the external condition of what I hold in the inner creative center of my being, I felt free.

Make the Effort...

Make the effort to clear your living space and discover yourself in a world of the present surrounded only by functionality. There will be nothing left to do tomorrow, no projects that remain for a rainy day; there will be only you and sleep and food and clarity. You will discover a guru of singular focus, ready to conduct the unseen forces of energy.

For example, a man I knew, Jacob, who could best be described as a playboy and who doesn't mind my describing him as such, eventually became enamoured with one woman. Unfortunately, she turned him down. Jacob knew in this moment that he wanted to settle down and start a family. So, he systematically went through his apartment and car and discarded absolutely everything that was not immediately useful. Three weeks later he welcomed into his life the woman of his dreams and all her "stuff."

When we engage in clearing, we see a physical representation of the organization or chaos of our thoughts. But we also, quite literally, make room for something new.

CLEARING IS A RITUAL OF COMMITMENT

Think of this act of clearing as your ritual of commitment, a commitment to welcome something new and better into your life. Here, you're taking a small step of letting go and burning the bridges that bind you to the same old way of being day in and day out.

It really only takes small steps to greatly affect your conviction, your beliefs, your imagination and inner trust in yourself.

For example, Yvonne needed money, but she was struggling to believe in good things for herself. She admitted that, deep down, she was plagued by doubt. Then she started clearing. As she did, she concentrated on welcoming money into her life. Yvonne started to feel a bit of a lift in her emotions right away. Later, she reported that as she was sealing up the first box of items for charity, she suddenly stopped and thought, "I must believe things will change, because I'm doing this." Yvonne was no longer just thinking about change, she was actively engaged in it.

The next afternoon she went for a short walk and met a couple from out of town. She started telling them about her life and how she was clearing out her apartment to bring about good fortune. They started discussing luck and the other woman suggested that they buy a couple of lottery tickets.

The next week passed somewhat uneventfully, and Yvonne's lottery ticket turned out to be a dud. However, the following week, Yvonne opened her mail and discovered a check for almost seven thousand dollars!

It turned out that the couple Yvonne met won a substantial sum of money on their lottery ticket and immediately sent off a portion of it to Yvonne, saying that they wanted to share a bit of their good fortune. Trust yourself! Clear the way for any and all new experiences you want to have in your life.

IDEAS TO ASSIST YOU IN CLEARING

Clear out any clutter around you and give yourself freedom of mind. In much the same way that you might start mentally decorating an empty room, you stimulate your creativity, excitement and positivity when you rid your life of old and excessive stimuli.

The following should assist you to de-clutter:

• Set a *clearing* schedule that you know you can keep, perhaps fifteen minutes each day. In this time, clear out one cupboard or one drawer or one box of papers.

• Here's a trick for clearing your clothes. Over the next month, every time you do laundry hang up the laundered clothing items. Use bags to hang up your laundered socks, underwear, nightclothes, nylons, sports gear, etc. Hang up everything: t-shirts and casual shirts, jeans and casual pants, dress shirts and dress pants, suits, and any jackets you wear.

At the end of the month, any clothing not hanging up is clearly clothing you don't wear on a regular basis or clothing that is seasonal. Discard, or aggressively sort through, the unused items. And if you still feel that you just might wear something, continue this exercise for the next couple of months.

You will likely find that there are only a few shirts, pants, sweaters and dressier items that you wear over and over while the rest of the clothing just sits there taking up space and energy.

You might also make it a rule that whenever you desire something new, you first discard something else, something you've grown tired of, that's worn out or out of style.

• In clearing your home, go room by room and empty a room completely. Take absolutely everything out and carefully consider each item you put back. Clear your car, office, purse or briefcase in the same manner.

Get a large box and label it "Charity." Place items you know you don't need, but just can't bring yourself to part with, in this box. When the box is full, close it up and seal it with tape. Put the box in storage, a spare room, or ask a friend if they can store it for you. In a few weeks, ask yourself, "Can I send this box to charity now?" You will likely find that, after you begin manifesting your goals and welcoming abundance and daily miracles into your life, you are no longer attached to many of the items you tucked away. Instead, you are likely to start eagerly clearing out even more stuff in anticipation of your new creations.

• If you already know what it is that you desire in life, ask yourself, "Does this item serve any purpose in the creation of my desire? Will it assist me to achieve my desire?"

• If you're not sure or you feel that you "just might" need an item in the future, ask yourself if the item can be replaced easily, borrowed from a friend or perhaps picked up for next to nothing at a second-hand store if you really do need it in the future.

• Clearing can be an extremely effective exercise for helping us identify some of our more dominant negative mental clutter, especially fears. If you are having trouble removing certain items, ask yourself, "Am I holding on to this item out of guilt? Why do I feel bad about removing an object? Do I fear something? What am I worried about? What is it that I worry will happen if I do get rid of this item?"

• Try to give everything a specific purpose and function. Instead of filling a cupboard shelf with glasses, cups and bowls, establish one shelf for cups, one for bowls, one for glasses. Consider how many items of a similar type you use in a day and how many of these items you need in a week. If you are keeping fifteen glasses, see if you can scale down, and perhaps keep eight, which serves a reasonable number of people and should be enough for your own use in a week. The idea is to simplify and limit everything for space and functionality.

• Make clearing a habit. Keep a small bag in your purse, pocket or briefcase and whenever you receive a receipt, place it in the bag and make it a habit to file or shred the contents each day or week. Create a filing system for your mail and schedule time to read through it, respond and pay bills. In small ways, make it a habit to welcome more energy into your life.

• This small, simple act of clearing will greatly affect your mental thought process. You will soon find that you are treating everything in your life in the same way that you treat physical clutter, asking yourself, "Does this help me or hinder me?" You start to become very strong about allowing only the most uplifting and rewarding people and events into your life.

REFLECTIONS ON STEP ONE
ONE-POINTED THOUGHT

Step One is the means to fully use and control the powerful energy of your thoughts, and it brings with it the benefits of knowing yourself better.

Through these simple and effective means, you lay the groundwork for the full construction of your desire. You are ensuring that you release only the most positive energy to consistently magnetize your life to abundance and reward.

The *Inventory Journal* in Step One exposes the thoughts that can potentially interfere with your ability to create. This is a first step toward achieving your desires, and so much more.

Clearing supports a clear and focused pattern of thought. With each act of clearing, you train and condition yourself to anticipate similar benefits as you later carry out the same actions on a mental level, replacing useless mental clutter with purposeful thought.

And as you are a vessel for energy, both exercises free up and increase your capacity to give and receive energy.

Having completed Step One, you should be aware of some of the more predominant barriers to your creative power. You have also established the benefit of increasing the flow of energy into your life. And you have carried out a mental and physical ritual that demonstrates to you that you truly believe in your creative power. And more than that, you are anticipating, and willing to accept, the goodness and bounty in life you're entitled to.

Step One will bring a sense of clarity and organization to both your thoughts and living space. It will feel like you have prepared a clean slate on which to write your life. You will feel ready to go, energized and full of anticipation over what will fill the new spaces in your life.

You are now ready to purposefully create and to define the first thing you want to manifest in your life.

STEP TWO
desire

*Desire is the serum of the soul,
secreted to the universe in thought,
binding the energies of creation—
form given genesis in one's own image.*

I AM
I am what I will
I will what I believe
I believe what I accept
I accept what I love
I love what I am
I AM

PRINCIPLES
ORGANIZATION & EVOLUTION

Your next step is to discover your *desire*, which is what you truly want to experience in your life, *right now*. Your desire can be for something physical, emotional, mental or spiritual. You may desire riches, happiness, peace of mind or the discovery of your higher self and purpose. *All of which you deserve!*

Desire is a powerful emotion. You could spend years training yourself to tap all the right emotions and formulate just the right pattern of thinking to release your full creative potential, but when you express desire you automatically assemble four dynamic emotions: *Will, Faith, Expectation* and *Love.*

Therefore, to say that your next step is to discover your *desire* is really to say that your next step is to discover your *will, faith, expectation* and *love*. And even more so, you want to nurture and expand these elements within you.

Desire, then, is both an objective and a process. It gives your thoughts a focus—a target to which you'll aim every arrow of thought. At the same time, it describes a particular way of organizing your thoughts. In other words, desire describes both a process of organization and the pattern that results.

Thus, a central theme of Step Two is *organization*, which is all you need to plant the seed of creation. When you organize your thoughts, you simultaneously organize the energy around you to form as the specific things you think about. This is something you are doing even now, though perhaps less consciously. As a result, the energy around you responds to the organization you project onto the world most often—the things you believe deeply and focus on, again and again.

Here, in Step Two, as with all the steps, we want to take conscious control of the process. As such, it's useful to begin by understanding how the process works.

Therefore, in the following principles we'll look at a description of the four dynamic elements of desire that describe the particular way in which desire organizes our thoughts and energy. We'll also look at the distinctive effects that result from the organization of our thoughts. Specifically, we'll look at two further effects of energy: the *Principle of Organization* and the *Principle of Evolution*. Together, these principles explain how desire works, how it moulds and shapes the conditions of your life. Finally, we'll explore the essential nature of desire, because it truly reflects the essence of our ability to create. This will help us to better understand how to formulate and express our desires.

By the time you finish reading the principles of Step Two, you'll be ready to embark on a journey of discovery to find out what experiences you truly want to have in your life, right now. You'll be ready to learn how to ask for what you want. And as you do, you'll be able to clearly picture how your every thought is moulding and shaping the conditions of your life to bring you the experiences you desire.

THE FOUR DYNAMIC ELEMENTS OF DESIRE: WILL, FAITH, EXPECTATION & LOVE

Think of will, faith, expectation and love as the ingredients of desire. If you want to experience desire in your life, you need to give yourself the ingredients to make it. Perhaps at times in your life you couldn't figure out what you desired. But in all fairness, how could you? You need first to familiarize yourself with its necessary ingredients. You want to know your will, faith, expectation and love.

Of course, by the same token, you may have had the experience of getting what you want, only to discover that you didn't really want such a thing. Here again, it's important to familiarize yourself with the ingredients of desire. Think about it like cooking. If you use sugar in the recipe and you like sugar, it's a safe bet you'll like the sweets you're baking. The same is true of your desires. If you familiarize yourself with the ingredients, you'll be sure to enjoy your desires, because whatever your desires, they will simply be a particular expression of your will, faith, expectation and love.

And of course, if you gather more ingredients, you can make more and greater things. Therefore, you want to nurture and expand these dynamic elements within you so that you can create a greater and more expansive reality for yourself.

By taking the time now to clearly understand the elements of desire, you will be able to recognize each within you and work on expanding them in the Method that follows. You'll recognize when your thoughts are truly creative as opposed to mere wishful thinking or hope. And if you ever find yourself struggling or feeling disconnected from your creative source, you can identify the elements blocked by clutter and effectively use the tools in the Practice, particularly in the following Method, to bring yourself back to an expression of desire and a truly creative mindset.

The First Element of Desire is Will

Will is your freedom to choose. It's what sets humans apart from all other creatures.

To choose means to desire one thing over another. When you select a desire, you let go of all other alternatives. For example, if you desire wealth, you see no other alternative and will accept nothing less. You cannot will for rich and still accept poor. You may choose one and then the other, but not both at the same time. Likewise, if you desire a beautiful home, all other options fall away and you can no longer entertain ideas or images of a lesser accommodation.

Therefore, hand-in-hand with *will* is *acceptance*. You must completely accept what you want. Acceptance means to see your desire as suitable, normal or usual. If you will to be rich, you must accept the idea that wealth is suitable for you, befitting your life, and in no way extraordinary or ridiculous. If you will for money but can't see yourself as rich, then it's no longer a desire; it's merely playful thinking.

Being willing to accept what you want sounds pretty simple, I know. If you want something, you're obviously willing to receive it and see it as fitting into your life. However, one of the first things you may notice as you come to define your desire is that, at a less conscious level, you may not be willing to see your desire as acceptable in your life. A host of conflicting thoughts and emotions may start surfacing.

You may hear in your mind all the reasons you can't have your desire—why it's not normal for you, why you don't deserve it. You might hear things like: "That won't really happen. You're not suited to that. It just isn't you. You've tried and failed before. You're too stupid, too old. You're just dreaming. Try something else. When was the last time you finished anything you started? People will laugh.

What will your friends say? There isn't enough to go around. Love isn't for you. There's no such thing as right work, just hard work and no one is happy anyway. You can't make money being creative. You should want more spirituality, not material things. You know it can't be done, right? You're dreaming way beyond your means, it's ridiculous. It's *impossible.*"

As you focus on your desire, monitor your thoughts. Be cognizant of whether or not your underlying thoughts and emotions are competing with your desire. Consider if you are willing pain, suffering and unhappiness into your life.

To will and accept negativity for ourselves is to give it to all. Instead, we want to contribute positively to our shared pool of energy. *Creation is not only a personal challenge and power, but also a collective responsibility.*

If you feel yourself struggling to maintain your desire, remind yourself that the conditions of your life are formed by the thoughts and emotions you exercise often and believe most deeply. Therefore, choose your desire, your will, carefully: "Thy will be done." When you will a thing, you set up a pattern of action in your mind and reaction in the world. Your will determines the energy around you, which in turn steers your life in a directed search for the opportunities for energy to reproduce.

Simply, when you express your will, the course of your life is set until you determine otherwise.

The Second Element of Desire is Faith

Obviously, to choose something and accept it is to believe in it. You must absolutely believe in your desires and in your power to manifest your desires. There is no point in saying, "I desire or I will" while in the back of your mind you're thinking, "I hope it to be true." Faith is stronger than hope. Faith knows that what you desire *is*, not that it can be.

> If you have faith, and doubt not...all things, whatsoever ye shall ask in prayer, believing, ye shall receive. – Matthew 21:21

For example, to say that one has faith in God or Infinite Intelligence is not to say that one has faith in the possibility of God or hopes that it's true. Faith is absolute. No evidence is required.

Faith also implies worthiness and trust. What you choose is a reflection of your self worth and your trust in yourself and the abundance around you. When you choose more, you express that you have faith in more. You express that you accept all things of worth as being suitable for you and others.

It is no exaggeration when we say that faith can move mountains. Faith has reshaped our world time and again. Faith accepts something as being so and we thereby think accordingly and literally bring it into being.

When you have faith in something, you simply do not accept evidence to the contrary. For example, not long ago, a discussion of sound waves would have been met with ridicule. Picture a faithful scientist presenting to a room of onlookers what he "knows" is true: that sound is the result of invisible waves that move outward to be received and interpreted. Our scientist is met with a room full of criticism and derision: "I'll get my umbrella, look out for the wave!"

Thomas Edison is often reported to have made 9,999 attempts to create the light bulb before he discovered the filament that produced light. Everything achieved is first mentally conceived with unrelenting faith. And if we believe in the impossible we shall see that come to pass as well. Henry Ford said, "Whether you think you can or you can't, you're right!"

When you express your will and stay faithful, knowing absolutely, "Thy will be done," you elicit your creativity. You broaden and intensify the waves of energy radiating from your mind. You command the forces around you to shape according to the form of your faith.

The Third Element of Desire is Expectation

Express your will, believe in what you will and *expect* it.

A woman bought into a lottery pool at work. Every day she said, quite matter-of-factly, "I imagine I'll get a check." She was simply expecting a material representation of what she already knew to be true. Soon after, she became one of several co-workers to share in a windfall of several million dollars.

Expectation is a positive, energizing, yet calming emotion in which you think and believe that something will come to pass. You're not hoping and wishing that something will happen, you know it will.

It is this inner "knowing" of unshakeable assurance that defines expectation. Expectation is a function of acceptance. You accept that your desire "is," and while this fills you with excitement, it also instills a seemingly incompatible state of peace, because you know that the result is assured. You experience all the agitating, stimulating and energizing emotions that accompany anticipation, but you identify with these states in a positive way and label them as excitement, confidence and peace. In other words, whatever agitation you might feel along the way, it is labeled "expectation."

Think of the alternative. In a journey to our dark side, we would tend to label agitation as fear, worry or anxiety. These emotions lower the vibratory state of our energy and isolate us from the source of universal energy and our own creative, imaginative and intuitive faculties.

The next time you feel agitated, say to yourself, "I'm just excited. I'm anticipating the material expression of my desire. I know my desire is on the way, good things are coming to me and I'm experiencing a sense of anticipation and expectation for what I know is true." You will immediately experience a sense of connectedness and feel your energy jump to a higher vibration.

Expectation is a powerful state. And what you pour into the energy around you comes back to you with greater force.

The Fourth Element of Desire is Love

Your desire should elicit in you feelings of love, which may be expressed as happiness, joy, giving, excitement, passion, sharing or a sense of connectedness.

Think about the sensations you experience when you turn your thoughts to a loved one. Or think about the sensations that accompany a first kiss. Or, imagine something you love to do like skiing, cycling, reading or writing and hold in your mind the sensations you associate with love.

Love is a very distinct and powerful energy that quickly transports our energy to a higher level.

For just a moment, close your eyes and try to picture the energy of love. Imagine a glowing cloud of light around the area of your heart. Give it a pinkish color like you might see at sunset. Now picture someone you care for in your mind and imagine sending this hazy cloud of light to float away from you to surround the other person.

Now do the same for yourself. Although, this time, imagine the energy near your heart spreading out to surround you. Imagine the energy soaking into your skin. Imagine yourself breathing it in. When you no longer wish to hold on to this image, pull the energy into your body and open your eyes. Memorize the sensations of warmth and goodwill you experience.

Memorize every experience of love. Live to see the experience of love flow outward from you at all times and to all persons. Love sets up a vibratory action in your consciousness that reaches beyond the speed of light.

By combining the energies of *will*, *faith*, *expectation* and *love*, you weave a pattern of one-pointed, pure thought called desire.

How Desire Works:
Organization & Evolution

Now that you have an understanding of what desire is and you've had a chance to read through the elements of desire that show the powerful way in which desire assembles your thoughts and energy, we can look at how desire works.

Specifically, we'll look at two further principles of energy: *organization* and *evolution*. Together, these principles explain how desire generates matter and the experiences you want to have in your life.

The Principle of Organization

As we know, everything is energy and there are many different types and grades of energy: air, heat, water, light and all sorts of infinitesimally small atoms, molecules, and particles that make up the various things in our world. But despite the many kinds of energy, at the heart of all things, even the tiniest atom, is the same basic creative energy.

To help give imagery to this invisible reality, take a moment to look at something around you, like this book, a cup or an apple, and imagine that within and around it you can see a very fine, vibrating "cloud": a subtle field of energy.

Einstein, in his unified field theory, referred to such a basic creative field as a *master field*. I have also seen it called an *organizing energy field,* which makes sense, because it's a subtle intelligence that attracts and organizes energy into particular shapes and sizes. It's rather like the DNA in our bodies, which functions as a blueprint or subtle intelligence instructing our cells to form and function in various ways.

This creative field of energy acts as a conduit or link between the higher, subtler energy of creation and the denser, more compact, physical manifestations of energy. It continually attracts higher-level energy, which is easily transformed, and directs it to condense and evolve into the qualities needed to create and supply the physical form.

For example, the creative energy within the human form is sometimes referred to as an energy body. We might also call it our consciousness, spirit, essence, higher power or soul. It's this subtle energy of our true being that links us with the higher energy of creation and all things. And it continually attracts, organizes and conditions energy to sustain and repair our physical form.

We can actually see such energy in energy photography or Kirlian photographs. These photographs record energy on film, causing it to appear as an "aura" or a halo of light, like the rays of the sun.

What makes such fields especially interesting to us in this Practice is that they exist prior to the creation of form or physical body. Einstein was adamant in saying that it's the field of energy that *creates* the form and not the other way around. In other words, a human being or an apple doesn't generate its creative field of energy. Quite the opposite. The energy field exists independently of, and prior to, the physical form.

Again, we can see this if we cut a leaf in half and take a Kirlian photograph of its energy. The photo will show an energy pattern of the complete leaf, because the creative energy of the leaf, which is responsible for organizing and maintaining energy in that particular form, still exists.

To summarize, an organizing energy field is a subtle field of energy and intelligence that exists before, during and after the physical form. It's a living blueprint or creative life force that guides energy to flow into a particular pattern to eventually evolve in physical form.

THOUGHT AS AN ORGANIZING ENERGY FIELD

Thought is a sort of "Grand Master" of all organizing or master fields. Our thoughts generate a subtle field of creative energy that can carry any pattern or design, depending on the idea or image in our mind. This mental energy then acts as a template or magnetic blueprint, organizing the energy around us into the pattern of our desire, eventually manifesting as the people, events and objects we want in our lives.

Remember, every thought is released as an impulse of energy. The energy carries the qualities, instructions or details of our thoughts, much like our DNA carries the plans to create our form.

Many of our thoughts are fleeting or somewhat vague, so the energy only carries the general quality of our thoughts as either positive or negative, raising or lowering the overall vibration of our energy accordingly.

However, when we keep the majority of our thoughts positive, our energy becomes highly vibratory, fine and subtle, immediately attracting to the same quality of energy in all things—the basic creative energy we all share. *And,* if we now introduce a clear and specific thought, we send out specific qualities, details or instructions to the fine layer of energy that runs through all things. As such, we immediately begin to organize the energy around us into the pattern of our desire, drawing into our lives the things we want.

> Remember, every thought is released as an impulse of energy. The energy carries the qualities, instructions or details of our thoughts, much like our DNA carries the plans to create our form.

In other words, when you project a clear and specific desire from a foundation of positive thought, it's as if you are standing on a balcony, shouting out to the entire world exactly what you want.

Imagine calling out, "I desire a car." Someone might respond and offer to give you a car. Someone else might shout, "I have what you want," and you are now urged to move in a specific direction to fulfil your desire. Or you may set up a chain reaction. Someone might suddenly have the idea to give away a car, perhaps as a sort of lottery, and someone else shows up at your door selling lottery tickets and a visiting friend buys you a ticket and you win the car.

Thought is essentially an organizing energy field on a grand scale, attracting, organizing and evolving a vast network of energy.

Thought is a living blueprint that moulds and shapes the subtle substance that makes up our world.

THE PRINCIPLE OF EVOLUTION

Remember, too, that organizing energy fields are like conduits or links, continually attracting available energy and transforming or evolving it to the physical level.

We can follow the transformation or evolution of energy in particle tables in science texts. These tables simply describe how small particles of energy attract, organize or collect together and grow into larger, more stable forms of energy.

For example, in the lepton family of particles, a *pion*, existing just below the speed of light, absorbs energy and becomes a *muon*. A *muon* absorbs energy and grows, and so on. Eventually, we have *electrons* and particles we are more familiar with.

You can think of the evolution of energy like a snowball rolling down a snowy hill. As the snowball gathers more and more snow it becomes larger, slower and more stable. Similarly, energy absorbs energy and grows and collects together, until eventually, it grows into the more stable energy that makes up physical matter and manifests on a perceptible level.

Thus, when we direct our thoughts inward to an emotional, mental or bodily level, our thoughts can quickly attract, organize and evolve or transform the energy around us into the specific qualities for our physical forms and we immediately begin to heal and energize our minds and bodies.

This explains many of the miracles in everyday life, such as why a frail, elderly woman was able to lift the front end of a car to free her trapped son following an accident. Or why many individuals diagnosed with a terminal illness have been able to vanquish their diseases through the power of thought.

Simply put, thought energy connects us with the subtle energy of creation, which we can then organize and condition for our use. We can, for example, supply the organizational fields of a group of cells within our body with enough energy to reverse and repair any damage, disorganization or "dis-ease" within the system. We can also super-charge a given system and experience what seems to be superhuman strength.

This interplay of science and spiritual dynamics explains why meta-physicians and practitioners of visualization have long held that a clear, positive and sustained thought will eventually evolve to manifest as physical materialization of energy, even in the absence of any direct physical action.

ASK AND YE SHALL RECEIVE

With the understanding you now have, let me return your attention to an earlier question, "What is desire?" The dictionary defines it as "an expressed request." Desire means *ask*. And as you can now see, desire is a *powerful mental request* that stirs into action the invisible forces that make the visible world possible.

THE ESSENCE OF DESIRE

Before you move on to the Method and begin to use desire to shape your life, it's useful to inquire into the nature of desire. This will help you to better understand why you desire something. And, ultimately, it will help you to see desire as an expression of the spirit.

To begin, let's compare desire with wanting. A want generally expresses what we *don't* have. If we say, "I want a car," we understand this to mean that we don't have a car, otherwise we would say, "I want a newer, sportier car." In fact, we often use the word want and need interchangeably. Often, "I want a car" could be just as well expressed as "I need a car." In other words, our wants tend to remind us of what we don't have in our lives.

And so, when we want things, it's often because we see ourselves as incomplete. Something's missing, so we believe we need things to complete us, to make us happy, successful, worthy, content, fulfilled.

As a result, we focus more on what we don't want in our lives. For example, we want money because we don't want to be a failure. We want a promotion because we don't want to be "nothing." We want a partner because we don't want to be lonely. Simply, we often want things because we're trying fix what we believe is missing or lacking in ourselves.

Of course, creation doesn't work this way, so we don't get what we want. And if we do manage to create, it comes at the end of a long struggle, and even then, we aren't at all happy or satisfied. We think, "I thought this would make me happy," or "I thought this is what I wanted." And this leads to more anxiety and greater fears. We think, "I'm afraid to make any more choices or try anything new, because every choice seems to be the wrong one." Then we think, "I'll never be happy." And then, "Something's wrong with me."

Creation doesn't work from a perspective of lack, because we're trying to fill a hole within us that doesn't exist.

Imagine if you stood in a garden with a shovel, attempting to fill a hole that wasn't there. What would happen? You'd end up with a pile of dirt. The same happens in our life when we needlessly try to fill a hole in us that simply doesn't exist.

However, even here our wants are an important part of our spiritual journey, because our struggles lead us to discover a better way, which is to discover what we do have and to express it.

And this is truly the essence of desire. Desire, unlike a want, is meant to be an expression of what we *do* have. In fact, in expressing our desires, we should see ourselves as artists. An artist identifies a feeling or image within and expresses it outwardly, giving it a particular representation, such as a painting or sculpture. The same is true when we express our desires. We identify creation within us and express it outwardly, giving it a particular representation, such as a car, better health or perhaps hearing our inner voice with more clarity. But whatever our desire, it is simply an expression of the abundance and love within us. It's an outward expression of what we already have in our possession.

> When you desire something, you are simply choosing to experience, now, what you already have.

Thus, in order to experience creation, we need to experience the realization that we are perfect, whole and complete, because creation is perfect, whole and complete and creation lies within us. The force of creation lies within all things and connects all things.

Therefore, everything you could ever want is already a part of you, physical or otherwise. Which means that you can never truly want for anything—"thou shall not want"—because you are already everything.

So, when you desire something, you are simply choosing to experience, now, what you already have.

Let me give you an analogy to make this clearer. Imagine that you have a huge bowl of every kind of fruit in the world and whenever you want an apple or a banana or the most exotic fruit, you simply reach out and help yourself.

Creation works the same way. You already have access to everything you could want inside you. And whenever you desire something, you simply extend the creative force within and experience what you will. In other words, our desires are simply a way of expressing the goodness and abundance of creation—the love, wealth, interest, success, enjoyment, talent and happiness—that we know exist within us.

For example, I desire a promotion because the new job will allow me to work with people, which I love. I desire money because I want to buy a house and decorate it. I believe I'm wealthy and I choose to express my wealth by buying a car, my favorite hobby. I desire a partner to share my love.

Desire is simply choosing something because it interests you, it's how you would like to express your creativity, it's what you want to share with others—and because, it's simply *a part of you, a part of creation,* that you would like to experience now.

Ask yourself, "Do I desire wealth because I believe I'm poor or something is missing within me? Or, do I desire wealth because I'm wealthy and I would like to concentrate my thoughts on the qualities and things that I believe express wealth?" "Do I desire happiness, because I believe happiness is not within me? Or, do I desire happiness, because I want to focus my thoughts on all the things I believe express happiness and fill me with energy?"

Desire expresses the abundant creative force already within yo fact, it's very much a tool to help you experience the spirit within and practise the basic spiritual tenet of being present in the moment.

When you desire something, you become very attentive to what fills your mind in each moment. You make conscious, purposeful, positive choices about what and how you think. You let go of any thoughts about past and future, which only exist in the imagination, and you focus solely on what *is*. And what *is* is what you think.

What you think, you create. What you think exists now, though it may not be immediately apparent. So, when you're thinking about your desire, you're focused on what *is*, here, in this moment. You're focused on what you believe, what you accept, what you love. And in each moment, you choose only the best experience for yourself.

Desires connect you with creation. They assist you to express your gifts. Your desires are simply particular representations of the spirit, like a painting or sculpture.

When you apply your gifts with integrity, there are no good or bad desires, no right or wrong choices. There are no mistakes, only experiences. If there is a concept of right or wrong in any sense, it is the difference between thinking and thinking with awareness. As long as you are thinking, you are creating and expressing the spirit. But, when you think with awareness you develop your gifts to create a more loving and joyous existence for all.

You should specifically create all that you desire, material or otherwise, and in so doing, discover something far more sublime. And as you easily manifest what you hold in your mind, creating money, a home, youth and vitality, you will inevitably seek more enduring creations that challenge and evolve your spirit and immerse you in something far greater than the physical experience. You will seek out contributions that lift, inspire and evolve all of humanity and keep you connected with the spirit, energy, God, or Infinite Intelligence, so that you can maintain the sublime and overwhelming sensation this brings.

It's so important that you feel comfortable to create. Release any mental constraints you may have imposed on your imagination and experience your natural abundant state. There are no limits to your creativity. Express your thoughts as if in a dream, where you are free to change events and objects and mould the conditions around you into unique expressions of joy, love and inspiration.

> When you apply your gifts with integrity, there are no good or bad desires, no right or wrong choices. There are no mistakes, only experiences.

Release your creativity. Enter this chapter filled with desire. It's your key to mental creation and, like every step in the Practice, it's the key to so much more.

METHOD
MANIFESTATION COLLAGE
& DETAILING

This Method will guide you through a process to discover the one thing on which you will focus your thoughts. Later, if you like, you can focus on several desires at a time.

Once you make your selection, you will create a *manifestation collage* and *detail* your desire, asking for what you want. You'll then complete a *desire statement* and formulate a clear and specific request. And you'll be given a daily practice to expand your will, faith, expectation and love.

WHAT DO YOU DESIRE?

At times, many of us have been unable to pinpoint our desires or even what we like.

I think about how many times I have wondered and worried about what I want, where I should be and what I should be doing. Even simpler, what do I like? What is the right job? Do I want to go back to school? Do I want to be healthy? Do I? Because I will tell you honestly now, I have had a number of illnesses that served as a convenient break from all these questions.

There are a number of reasons for being unable to pin down our desires. For one, we fear we might ask for the wrong thing. Perhaps in the past, we were disappointed when we finally got what we wanted. Sometimes we're simply afraid to start something new or we feel we don't deserve anything or shouldn't ask for more. Imagine! All this wasted energy when we can create and recreate as we desire.

If you feel any of these concerns now, take a moment to dump your fears, add them to your Inventory and make a conscious decision to leave behind any worry, doubt or guilt. The universe will hand you what is best for everyone concerned, if you let it.

If you feel that you want too many things, that's great, as long as you don't become concerned with your indecision. The process is enhanced because you have desires. Desire charges your energy no matter what you want.

If you don't know what you want, or you want a number of things at this point, the information that follows will help you select a focus for your Practice.

DISCOVERING YOUR DESIRE

All you need to start on your way to discovering your desire is scissors, tape and some old magazines. You don't have to spend a lot of money buying a stack of new magazines. Most likely, someone you know has a pile of latest-trends-fabulous-haircuts magazines they'd be happy to give you.

Gather up all the magazines you've collected and find a quiet place where you can relax and focus for fifteen minutes or so, uninterrupted.

Start flipping through the pages of the magazines and, as soon as an image catches your attention, brings good things to mind, excites you, elicits a sense of faith, expectation, love, longing or interest, cut or tear out the picture and place it to one side.

This should be a thoroughly enjoyable experience in which you simply let your imagination run wild as you cut out images that pique your interest or infuse you with a jolt of positive energy.

By going through the magazines slowly and deliberately, selecting photos that inspire you and mean something to you, you will be surprised at just how easily you can identify people, objects and events of interest.

You may find that several pictures interest you, although none really seem to be a definitive desire. Or it might happen that you feel torn between two seemingly opposing desires. For example, you desire to live in Florida and you would also like to live in Europe. Don't be concerned with your indecision. Cut out everything of interest.

If it happens that nothing in particular strikes your fancy, try to select images that represent the different areas of your life. Think about the physical, mental, emotional and spiritual areas. You might cut out a diamond or a home to represent wealth, love or family, or find pictures of athletics to represent something physical. You might cut out food to reflect health, educational pictures to reflect intellectual endeavours or inspiring words that serve to express the spiritual aspect of your life.

To assist you, consider the following areas of your life in which you can express your power of creation:

- The desire to express wealth, riches, fulfillment and success.

- The desire to express health, youth and vitality.

- The desire for emotional expression: joy and happiness.

- The desire for friends and social connections.

- The desire for love, a life partner, marriage, children, a home.

- The desire for artistic endeavours and expression.

- The desire for work and the right arena to express your talents.

- The desire for spiritual awareness and cosmic connection.

MAKING YOUR DESIRE VISIBLE

When you finish going through the magazines or feel that you have enough pictures, take all of your images and arrange them on a wall you see most often. You may wish to create your wall album beside your bed or in the room where you spend most of your time. You may even wish to create several collages in different rooms. Tape the pictures together and take care to place them so that only those images that interest you or you wish to see manifest are visible.

At this point, your collage is a representation of desire. It does not have to be the "be all and end all" of your final destiny. It is a collection of what attracts you, inspires you and brings you enjoyment. These are pictures that elicit in you a sense of will, faith, expectation and love.

This activity may seem like a small step. But how many times do we fail to take any steps? We must learn to crawl before we can walk. Small steps lead to bigger actions. Desire is the spark that ignites your creative faculties. Each positive emotion you experience in thinking about your collage weaves for you a pattern of thought that opens up your creative channels.

You will begin to experience a heightened awareness in imagination, intuition and inspiration, the three sisters of creation, as well as experiencing ideas, innovations and possibility. By bringing the dynamic elements of desire into your life, you align yourself more and more with one-pointed pure consciousness, and ignite waves of energetic attraction that will lead you to a healthy, wealthy and successful life.

SELECTING A DESIRE

Take time to enjoy the pictures you've cut out. When you feel ready, select one interest or area of your life to become the focus of your Practice. It doesn't matter which. You will use this image or idea to continue the Practice. In other words, if you do not as yet know your desire, select an interest or even a "like" and treat it as though it were a true desire.

As you work with this interest, your true desires will begin to make themselves known. There will come a moment when you will be directed internally to one desire in particular, something that your mind continually keeps coming back to. It may be a particular picture from your collage or something new. But it will be a desire that you just *know* is important to you.

In fact, even at this stage, as you work through this chapter, you will likely find that you are suddenly struck with an overwhelming desire or new idea.

If you like, you can choose a different area of interest every few days. But until you decide on the one thing you want to manifest, it's a good idea to stay with one image for at least a couple of days before moving on to another area of interest. Simply continue to repeat all the steps in the Practice until you *know* the one desire you want to focus on and manifest.

Keep in mind that you don't have to concern yourself with how your desire will come about. Even if you don't know what you want, trust in yourself and the process.

By choosing even one "lukewarm" desire on which to focus your Practice, you start to develop the dynamic emotions of desire: will, faith, expectation and love. More importantly, you construct a positive pattern of one-pointed thought by keeping your mind actively engaged with a single, positive objective. In doing this, you are developing the elements that will lead you to *know* your desire.

The more you work with each step, the more your creative faculties take over. Soon you will leap from rationality to an experience of knowing. Immerse yourself in the Practice; you will receive inspiration and intuitive guidance as you do.

CREATE A MANIFESTATION COLLAGE

At this point, you will create a collage focusing on the one desire you wish to manifest. (Remember, choose even a lukewarm interest at this point and you'll be pleasantly surprised at how this one small step will stimulate your creativity, stretch your imagination and quickly and easily lead you to *know*.)

There are a few things to keep in mind as you begin to select the images that will make up your manifestation collage. The pictures should be color and as "real" as possible. The images are best if they are concrete, not abstract. An image of the thing itself, the object or event, works better than an image that is only symbolic or representative or your desire. For example, if you desire a home, select pictures that closely resemble the exact exterior or interior you want, rather than a picture of a heart that represents the idea of home to you, as in "home is where the heart is."

If your desire is somewhat abstract, such as peace, your images may in fact be more metaphorical. But consider cutting out words that are concrete, such as "Peace," or a poem or image that is clearly symbolic to you, like angels, a ray of light or a serene image of a mountaintop. In other words, be creative. Include symbols and pictures that elicit emotion, but as much as possible, visually depict your desire exactly as you would like to experience it.

For example, if you desire a car, try to find a picture of the exact car in the exact color you want and with a clear insignia and the brand name spelled out across the page. If you desire a home, find a picture that resembles your dream as closely as possible. If you desire more clients for your business, find pictures of people and label them "buyer" or "client." Include pictures of yourself selling your product or delivering your service.

You may choose one image, or several. You might select a dominant picture—for example, the outside of your desired home—and give it a central focus by placing it in the center of your collage. You can then add pictures all around it depicting each room, the exact appliances you desire, the furniture, the carpets and draperies, etc.

Or, if you desire money, you might write out a check to yourself in the exact amount you desire. If the money is the result of a salary increase, you might add related pictures, such as a pay stub that you create to show how your requested sum breaks down biweekly and with deductions. You might add an employment offer by creating a letter to yourself that states your name, the title you desire, salary, hours of work and benefits.

Other examples of concrete pictures you might select are a diamond ring or a sandy white beach with the location written on the page. You may find a bright, smiling face, much like you desire for yourself, free of pain and blossoming with relief. You may choose to cut out a picture of a beautiful couple or clip out words like "sold," "life" and "health." You might choose pictures of individuals engaged in particular professions: ballroom dancer, writer, business owner, stenographer, artist, casino dealer, mother, police officer, homemaker.

If you think of any ideas for which you can't find images, create some. You might draw an image or use a computer to download or create an image. There may be an object you have that you can use to represent your desire. Or you can use a photo, new or old, which may be one of your own or borrowed.

Have fun with this exercise and find different ways to create detailed images of your desire. You might create your collage in a frame that is portable and can be set up in any room. You can display your pictures on a corkboard, in a binder or paste them into a journal. You may even want to create smaller collections: photo-albums or pocket-sized reminders.

The end goal is to create as detailed a representation as you can and to make sure that you see this visual presentation of your desire every day, morning and night and as many times as possible throughout the day. (You can also record your desires and listen to them on tape).

The key is to keep your thoughts and emotions focused on the essence of your desire and, as much as possible, continuously direct the energy of your thoughts toward a specific objective.

An Illustration ~ The Power of A Picture

One woman decided to focus on a small reward, a ring, something she had always wanted to buy for herself.

She found five pictures that showed rings covered in diamonds. She also drew a picture of her desired ring that had a green stone in the center, which she felt was a beautiful and precious representation of life.

Several days later, she found a picture in the newspaper that showed a gorgeous antique gold ring, almost an inch in width, that featured a green center stone with diamonds all around it. She cut out the newspaper photo and carried it in her wallet.

Two weeks later, a friend asked if she would run an errand for her. She was asked to purchase a number of jewellery items as gifts for clients. She selected the gifts and, a week later when she visited the jeweller to pick up the items she had ordered, the jeweller's wife gave her a nudge and wink and handed her a gift-wrapped box. Inside was a lovely ring with a diamond in the center. The woman was shocked and assumed this gift was the manifestation of her desire.

However, several weeks after that, friends invited her for lunch and handed her a jewellery box. It contained a handcrafted ring, virtually identical to the newspaper photo. She hadn't shown the photo to anyone and had never mentioned her desire. She immediately went home and took down the pictures of rings and started her next, greater desire.

I should mention that this is a story I know quite well, since it is my own.

DETAILING YOUR DESIRE ~ A DAILY PRACTICE

Find time each day to sit down with a pen and paper and write out your desire beginning with the words, "I Desire" or "I AM." For example, you might write, "I Desire wealth" or "I AM healthy." You can also ask someone to assist you or use a recording device and speak your desire out loud.

Keeping your collage and desire in mind, continue to list as much detail as you can presently imagine about your desire. You can write out details in point form or create a story and write a narrative about your desire. Be sure to write about your desire using the present tense. For example, if you wrote down "I am living in my dream home," you might continue on to say, "The house sits on an acre of land near the ocean. The front door is red and upon entering the house I see a beautiful chandelier. The floor is made of marble..." and so on. Write about where the house is located and the date you *moved* in (remember, you already live there!) Do you have any pets? Is there a shed or fence on the property? How do you spend your days? What are you doing in the house? Who comes to visit?

Spend time really enjoying your desire in as much detail as possible, as though it is occurring or has already occurred.

You may wish to consider some of the following details. Included here are examples of money, health, romance, travel and work.

MONEY: If you want a large amount of money, decide exactly what bills you want and draw a picture of each bill. Have you ever seen a thousand dollar bill? What are the details on the bill? Be specific.

For example, not long ago, a few others and myself repeatedly drew pictures of money we desired. We continued this practice for several days, until we felt that we were already in possession of the money. Not long after, each of us attracted money into our lives, and in most cases, a great deal more than we had pictured.

Energy, remember, responds immediately to what you "put out there." You simply need to be specific and, more importantly, consistent.

You might calculate in as many ways as possible what the amount of money you are receiving looks like. How many suitcases would you need to accommodate such a sum? If you piled up the money in your living room, what would it look like? Could you cart it around in a car? Would it fill a bathtub?

If you desire a million dollars and have never seen such a sum, how can you fathom this figure? What does a million dollars look like? What will you do with it? What do things cost? Is it enough money? Why a million dollars? Why not more?

You might also think about how you want to receive the money. Do you want money from an innovation, a better job, a creative endeavour, recognition, fame or education? Would you like to make money by using your hands, or your mind?

Make a list of the things you envision yourself purchasing with the additional money you desire. Detail each purchase. Draw or cut out pictures of your purchases.

Consider how you will share your money. Whom might you assist?

List what things look, feel, taste and smell like. Explore every avenue you can imagine.

HEALTH: What does health look like to you? Think of the things you are doing with your increased energy and vitality. Picture the inner workings of your body and make detailed lists commanding the cells, blood and oxygen to perform as you desire.

Let me share a brief story to assist you in this regard. When I started this Practice, I was very ill. I was losing my hair. The glands in my throat were grotesquely swollen and my hands were painfully enlarged. My face was covered in sores. I ached all over. I suffered incredible headaches and nausea and I was profoundly tired. I hesitate to write more, as I am now keenly aware of the power of what I express. So, suffice it to say that my immune system had decided to take leave of its senses.

Nonetheless, I forced myself to pick up a pen and paper and detail my health. Fifteen minutes later I felt urged to draw a picture of myself expressing happiness and health. I can't say the picture was all that great, but it seemed important that I draw it.

About a half hour later, after I had finished writing, friends arrived. When I opened the door I was met with shocked faces and outbursts of, "Oh my!" My friends shuffled me into the bathroom, urging me to look in the mirror. I did. My face had begun to heal.

It took very little time to heal after that. And, of course, I have since had the pleasure of sharing this Practice with many others whose experience has been the same.

Synthia, for example, instructed her body to rid itself of gallstones. She made out detailed lists telling her body to concentrate on dissolving the crystallized fat in her gallbladder. At night, she spoke out loud, giving instructions to her body on how to repair itself. She told her body that she would provide the necessary diet and energy to be converted for each instructed purpose.

Synthia felt better immediately. Within days she became aware that her body was excreting small, crystallized stones. The doctor confirmed that her body was processing the stones and voiding them.

If you don't feel well enough to write, talk to your body.

And remember, what you have in your life is simply an expression of what you hold inside. So love even the negative things you hold inside you that come to be outwardly expressed. Your barriers and challenges are part of your growth. They are gifts. Thank them and choose to move on.

ROMANCE: Remember Elena's story? Over the course of several weeks, she wrote out copious detailed lists describing her future mate.

Consider the things you and your dream partner do together. What does your soulmate do for work and fun? What activities does your soulmate enjoy? Where does you partner live? What does your partner say? What are the exact words you like to hear your partner say to you? Consider smells, like the exact perfume or cologne they use, if any.

Make a note of any preferences you have. Does your soulmate have an accent? Imagine their dress, appearance and mannerisms. Image the person's gait and stride. Are they tall or short? Note any particular phrases that are unique to this person. Notice actions that appeal to you. List hobbies and particular interests they have.

TRAVEL: List the details of the place or places you are visiting. Keep an imaginary diary of your adventures. Make very specific notes about the people you are meeting and what you are doing and what you eat and see.

WORK: What work are you engaged in? If you are not sure what work is right for you, list individual tasks that you enjoy doing. Do you work inside or out? Do you work with others or alone? What do you wear to work? Do you work with your hands or equipment of any kind? What hours do you work? What do you earn? Are there any bonuses attached to the job? What are the benefits? Do you travel? Is your work close to home? Are there any interesting courses you might take relative to your job?

Detailing your desire is a positive form of journaling and should be a thoroughly enjoyable experience that feels completely real, as though you are actually living your desire.

> Write everything down as though your desire has actually occurred or is occurring. Live the experience.

Each time you engage your mind in the details of your desire, you actively exercise one-pointed thinking, keeping all your thoughts and emotions focused toward a single, positive objective that will quickly evolve to a *habit* of positivity. You stimulate the appropriate emotions: will, faith, expectation and love. You awaken your intuitive faculties. And you command energy to work as you desire.

Keep in mind also that we are conditioned to believe what we see and hear. Writing out the details of our desires gives them a sense of reality. And by reading our desires out loud, verbalizing our plans, hearing them, we give them a sense of action and bring them to life.

Carry out this exercise randomly throughout the day, whenever you have a few minutes.

Your Desire Statement

You can now use the details you have created to rewrite your desire and formulate a more specific request—a desire statement—a clear, energizing statement that you can recall, repeat and reflect on throughout the day.

Think of your desire statement like a plan for building a house. It would do no good to say to an architect, "I want a house." You need to provide details. In the same way, you are the architect of your life and need to provide the universe with the specific details that bring your idea into form. Don't concern yourself with "how" or "when" your desire will manifest. Simply create detailed statements that describe the perfect outcome.

For example, your written desires might evolve from general desires, such as "I desire money" or "I desire a car," to more specific desires, such as "I desire a raise of ten thousand dollars" or "I AM earning X dollars a year" or "I desire a new red sports car" or "I am finishing a course in art appreciation and have been offered a job with a prestigious art gallery for a yearly income of fifty thousand dollars." This last example is in fact the desire one woman wrote down and received. She now travels to resource perspective artists, earning considerably more money than requested. She was forty-one and struggling to find a job when she wrote this desire on paper.

It may help you to create a more specific desire statement if you imagine yourself speaking with a friend. Discuss your desire, in mind or out loud.

Remember, you have the ability to project into the outer world what you will, but you must first imprint a clear mental image onto your thoughts. The creation of form is almost automatic after that.

Know, also, that when you express your request and ask for what you will, you express your readiness to receive. This is important. Your desire statement says, "I acknowledge the power within me and, thus, the power in *all that is*. I trust in that power, and in my gift to extend such power, and so I express my will. I feel worthy and loved. I am ready to receive."

In other words, your desire statement is not tunnel vision. It is not saying, "I accept this and only this. I have closed my eyes and ears to the wisdom of the universe." Instead, your desire statement communicates your love, faith and readiness to work *with* the higher energy of the universe. When you speak or think your desire statement, you do so with complete trust that the universe will deliver what is best for all. You state it knowing full well that you may receive this or, as is often the case, something better.

THE GREATER YOUR MENTAL CONCEPTS, THE MORE EXPANSIVE YOUR REALITY

To refresh your mind, we are working with a simple metaphysical law: everything achieved is first mentally conceived.

Look around you. All the buildings, cars, planes—*all things*—were first ideas in the minds of people daring to stretch their imaginations beyond the apparent confines of their current conditions.

You can create whatever you can imagine and impress onto your consciousness. If you imagine more, you create more. And to imagine more, you need to exercise your imagination.

Each time you engage in the detail and design of your desires, you not only forge the conditions of your life, you exercise your imagination. You tap into the creative energy at the heart of you and access a limitless reservoir of possibility, knowledge and power, which you can use to expand on the concepts you hold about your self and your life.

And when you repeatedly expose yourself to new ideas and greater concepts, such thoughts become commonplace and acceptable in your life. You develop a rich consciousness. You naturally expect new and greater things for yourself.

Derrick and Eve, for example, were watching a television program about the world's most expensive real estate. At the end of the program, Derrick said, "Doesn't that make you feel insignificant?" Eve, who had been detailing her desire for several days, said, "That's not so much money. I can see myself winning that much money or earning it."

Everything achieved is first mentally conceived.

Interestingly, this comment was uncharacteristic for Eve, but her views had become increasingly more expansive through detailing, to the point that she could now see just how possible *everything* is. Consequently, she had begun to simply *allow* more into her life.

You will see your mental concepts growing each time you engage in the detail of your desire. And creating new and greater mental concepts is all you need to do to create a greater and more expansive reality for yourself.

However, at present, you may be experiencing constraints to your imagination. It's often here, as you progress through the Practice, that some of your more deeply rooted clutter may arise. It shows up specifically to weaken and limit your will, faith, expectation and love.

As a result, you simply may not imagine more for yourself or see something greater as *acceptable* and normal in your life. You may not *believe* in the things you are writing down and feel as though you're just "making things up" or being ridiculous.

It's important, therefore, to combine Steps One and Two. As you detail your desire, let your mental clutter signpost the way and tell you where to focus your attention and imagination.

To do this, write down the four elements of desire before you begin to detail: will, faith, expectation and love. Beside each, write out the things you can reasonably believe and expect at this time.

For example, you might write:

WILL: *I will for a partner.*

FAITH: *I believe I deserve to meet someone.*

EXPECT: *I expect I will meet someone, but maybe not right away. I expect them to be decent and kind.*

LOVE: *I love a lot of things about myself and I want to share them.*

When you have written out what you will, believe, expect and love, take note of any jailers or restrictive thoughts. Then, as you detail your desire, focus on specifically strengthening and expanding your will, faith, expectation and love.

In this example, write about what you like and love about yourself and expand on what you expect and believe you deserve.

You might repeat the same beliefs and expectations for a few days and then, when it feels comfortable to do so, see if you can stretch your imagination a little and expand your beliefs. You will likely discover that thinking more expansively takes little conscious effort the more you detail your desire.

For example, you might progress to write:

> *I could meet someone today, right away. Why not? I am ready for more, because I know I am more. I expect I will meet someone with the qualities I desire. I deserve more. Not because I work hard or do good things, but just because I am. I deserve to experience the best....*

You might continue in this vein for several days and then expand your thoughts even further and write:

> *I am perfect, whole and complete. I fill my thoughts with wonderful, beautiful images and ideas and contribute these feelings and energy to everyone. I expect to receive an abundance of joy in return. My partner will fill my life with new joys...*

You will be able to look back over your writings and actually see the progression of your thoughts to a more expansive view. You will see the barriers to your creative power dissolving quite magically. Limitations that once seemed overwhelming and real will now be the thoughts that seem ridiculous and illusory. And you will find that you can leave limiting beliefs behind as easily as you can flip the page and start writing anew. And one morning you'll wake up and think, "A million dollars? Why not fifteen million dollars? Anything is possible."

REGIME FOR BUILDING BIGGER MENTAL CONCEPTS

Remember, our best and most innovative ideas often come from our darkest challenges and difficulties. These can be life's greatest gift, for they urge us to think differently and greatly, if we are willing to look for what's possible.

Consider the following techniques for building new and greater mental concepts. Use each as you need and incorporate them into your detailing routine. (You may want to start a detailing notebook.)

START WITH SMALLER DESIRES. Desires you can believe and expect will lead you to slowly use your imagination to create greater faith and expectations. By exercising your imagination every day through continually detailing your desire, you will come to will, accept, believe and expect a great deal more for yourself.

Tim wanted a raise and was comfortable requesting and accepting five to eight thousand dollars, although eight thousand was a bit of a stretch in Tim's mind. As Tim wrote out the details of his desire, he started to believe that ten thousand dollars was quite acceptable and realistic and thought it could just as well be eleven or thirteen thousand. Two weeks later, Tim requested, and received, a raise just shy of thirteen thousand dollars. And just two weeks earlier, he would have requested and likely received five or eight thousand dollars less!

CREATE POSSIBILITY. Use your imagination to create ideas and scenarios where your desire can work and be believed. Simply, create possibility. For example, if you find it difficult to see yourself alone earning more money, imagine that everyone in the organization gets a raise. What if the money came as some sort of bonus?

Continue to write until you create a scenario that *feels* possible. It doesn't have to be the one you want at this time, but see how far you can push your imagination. Do the same for any aspect of your desire you find difficult to believe or expect.

Repeat this exercise often. Eventually, higher ideals and greater images start to become part of your regular thinking process and seem acceptable and normal in your life. And you will be surprised at how, quite "magically," your life soon starts reflecting what you think—greater possibilities.

For example, a young couple was looking for a home. The wife was dreaming about living in a wealthy area of town, which irritated her husband, who saw this desire as ridiculous and unrealistic. I suggested that they work together to create a collage and focus on seeing this desire as possible. I asked them to think about all the ways such a desire might come true. For example, someone might offer to give them a home. They might win a home in a lottery. They might find an excellent deal, perhaps a foreclosure. The husband finally agreed that there were plausible ways in which such a desire might come true. And with this seed of faith planted, the couple was able to concentrate on the details of their desire.

Sure enough, they found a deal. The home had been used for illegal purposes and they were able to purchase it for next to nothing. A few months later, after some elbow grease, they were living in their dream home, which had more than doubled in value.

CREATE DISTANCE. Whatever challenge or difficulty your mind poses, project the problem away from yourself and look at it as if you are watching a soap opera or movie, and then imagine solutions. Or, imagine that a friend is experiencing similar thoughts or feelings and has asked for your help, and then see how many possible solutions you can come up with. So often, when we are no longer dealing with our own limitations and personal fears, we can think more freely and speak from our creative center.

For example, Irene wanted to write a cookbook but she couldn't imagine how this would be possible. She didn't have much free time and she was discouraged thinking about the number of cookbooks already on the market. So Irene sat down and imagined what she might say to a friend or someone else with the same desire. This inspired her to write, "Do it anyway. Focus on what you love. You can only do right when you express love."

A week later, visiting a friend, Irene met a woman who publishes cookbooks. She agreed to help Irene compile and publish her book.

DECLARE YOURSELF WORTHY. As you detail your desire, focus on expressing *greater love for yourself.* Remember, your desires are a reflection of what already exists within you, and what exists within you is everything. But you need to accept this because energy can only work through you as much as you allow it to. Said another way, what you are willing to accept, and feel that you can handle, is exactly what life will hand you.

For example, John wanted to meet a woman and marry. He hadn't had too many good experiences with women and didn't think too highly of himself. He didn't believe in much and expected even less. He was simply hoping that he might meet a woman who would put up with him! Imagine! Each of us is so unique, a miraculous, powerful, sublime gift, connected to everyone, and yet we so often believe we are less. I certainly have. We need to remember that our thoughts can just as easily expand our experiences as they can limit us.

John, like many of us, needed to use his imagination to expand the concepts he held about himself—how much love he accepted and expected for himself. It took about three weeks for John to start dreaming a little bigger and detailing such things as, "I trust myself. My life counts." He rewrote his desire to read, "I desire a loving, confident woman, forty to fifty years of age, who enjoys outdoor activities."

A few days after he wrote out his request, John met a successful, forty-two-year-young woman who worked as a charity organizer and host. She was outgoing, athletic and talked John into yoga. And that was enough for John to ask her to marry him. The invitations were prepared to read, "We *Desire* your presence…"

SEE THROUGH LIMITATION. The only reason we experience limitations in reality is simply because we form limitations in our mind.

Joanna had created a mental ceiling on how much she could expect to earn. She used to think that if she could earn just forty thousand dollars a year, it would be truly miraculous. And she worked really hard to this end. She continually tried to upgrade her skills and compete for promotions.

Then Joanna met someone in the same line of work earning eighty thousand dollars a year. In that instant, Joanna's perception changed. All of a sudden, she could will for more because she could believe and expect it. Of course, her life immediately reflected her thoughts. A few days later, she was offered a job for seventy-odd thousand a year, with bonuses that would bring her salary to well over a hundred thousand a year.

Recognize that the only limits are those we self-impose, or more accurately, self-inflict. Immerse yourself in inspirational readings, music and relationships and nurture a consciousness of possibility and openness.

SEE THE WORLD ANEW. At odd moments throughout the day, choose something in your environment at random and mentally detail how it could be made better.

EXERCISE YOUR IMAGINATION. Consider using each idea or desire, even those you discard, as an exercise to expand your imagination. Follow through on an idea as far as you can so that you can say that it is completely possible, but that you have simply decided against it.

The more you work on creating positivity and seeing possibility and solutions, the more you can control your thoughts and emotions and establish one-pointed thinking. This control will enable you to release a steady stream of energy toward any objective, any time you want.

FOCUS ON YOUR DESIRE AS A TOOL TO REPLACE MENTAL CLUTTER

You now have several tools that you can use to replace and dissolve your mental clutter. Whenever you feel negative, distracting thoughts threatening your creative power, work on your collage, detail your desire and specifically concentrate on expanding your will, faith, expectation and love.

Don't compete against yourself by releasing opposing thoughts. Control the thoughts that occupy your mind. Negative and doubtful questions stretch time and keep you in the past or distant future. Learn through this practice to condense time and space. Be concerned only with the desires you decide are important and allow to exist in your mind now. Remember, the direction of your life is created with each thought.

Whenever your mind begins to incessantly puzzle on questions of "when" and "what if," such as, "When will I get my turn" and "What if it doesn't happen?" stop! Engage in the details of your desire, if only in mind, and believe, expect and love each thought. Think of this as your primary job in life. For any negativity that you allow to erupt, just as quickly give yourself one mental command, "Desire!" and turn your thoughts to the images you want in your life.

Tell yourself this: just do it once, just replace one negative thought, one time. Take one small step. And since there is no other time but this moment, if you do it, just this one time, right now, you've done it! This moment counts. It's the only one that counts.

Focusing on your desire is a "small step," a simple and conquerable task to caress and excite your consciousness with will, faith, expectation and love, in this moment and the next and the next. Give yourself a pure mental command of desire. Hold to this as the single most important job you do.

If you continuously come up against stumbling blocks to your will, faith, expectation and love, it may indicate several things.

You may be focusing on what you believe is lacking in your life. You may be purposely creating problems because, deep down, the thing you want is not something you are really in love with, it's simply a means to an end or it seems like the most plausible idea. Perhaps you feel you *should* want such a thing, because it seems like the "right" thing to do, the socially acceptable thing.

Sometimes we become so accustomed to negative thinking that it is simply automatic for us to create problems and not solutions. That's fine. This can be undone. But we must first notice limiting and destructive thoughts before we can replace them with solutions and possibility.

If you find yourself focusing on problems and disbelief, this may be an indication to go back and journal and dump a few more blocks and barriers. As you do, remind yourself that you can continue to keep your fears or you can thank them for stopping by and move past them.

As You Grow, Your Desires May Change

Don't be surprised if you find that you change your mind or alter your desire as you move through the steps in this Practice. You are increasing your awareness of your thoughts and emotions and heightening your creative and intuitive faculties. Changing and refining your desires is a natural part of the process.

Through this Practice, you will discover more clearly who you want to be, what you want in life, where you want to be and what you want to do. You will be exposed to completely new ideas as your imagination and concentration increase. And you are magnetizing your life to opportunities, "chance" meetings and other "coincidences" that can lead you in a completely new and rewarding direction.

> As your desires change, you are moving closer to your best life. Each step is a successful one.

Keep in mind that as your desires change, you are moving closer to your best life. Each step is a successful one. Remember, there are no mistakes, only experiences.

ILLUSTRATIONS

New Life Through Desire

You are everything that is, your thoughts, your life, your dreams come true. You are everything you choose to be. You are as unlimited as the endless universe. —Shad Helmstetter

One woman, Liza, immediately changed her life for the better by releasing the dynamic elements of desire into her life and building bigger mental concepts for herself.

I met Liza at a small dinner party. She was outgoing and personable. I commented to her that she had a wonderful personality and must be great with people. This caught her attention and she told me that it was true, but she was frustrated because, in spite of her rave reviews at work, she was paid very little. She wanted a new job and a substantial salary increase.

As it turned out, Liza was in the same line of work as Greg, who had escorted me to the party. Liza and Greg both worked in secretarial assisting positions, handling the same tasks, but Liza did a fair amount more than Greg. Liza managed the entire office, including some rather finicky and complicated legal filings, public relations and meeting and travel arrangements. Greg was an engineering secretary and Liza's role was described as reception. Greg earned considerably more than Liza and did considerably less. The difference lay in their imaginations.

Liza needed to expand her vision. She was limiting herself with the title of "receptionist" and her own derogatory descriptors of that role as lowly and insignificant. I saw her performing the functions of an executive-level secretary with a salary of at least $20,000 more than she currently earned. Liza dreamed of such a salary, but deep down, she couldn't see this as a reality for herself. I couldn't imagine less and Liza wouldn't imagine more.

I asked her to sit down with me and make out a plan for her dream job. When we began, she started with the title of receptionist and couldn't imagine more than a hundred dollars a week increase in pay. With the recounting of each work experience, Liza started to expand what she saw as possible for herself. She started imagining an increase of two hundred dollars a week. As this became realistic for her, she envisioned an even greater salary. We changed her dream job title to "Executive Assistant to the President." Liza started describing how the interview would go and began a job search for executive-level positions.

The following day, Liza was pouring herself a glass of milk and dropped the carton on the floor. Fortunately, she had another carton but, although it was days before the expiry date, the milk had soured. Liza walked to a corner store and, while in line at the register, started chatting with the woman behind her. The woman turned out to be a recruiter for a major firm and offered Liza an interview. Liza was hired for the position of Executive Assistant to the Chief Financial Officer, with a salary of $22,500 more than she had previously earned.

The Desirable Gift

A young couple became engaged. They had very little money, but they decided to take a portion of their savings and treat themselves to an expensive dinner. During dinner, the woman asked the server for a pen, and on a napkin the couple started detailing their desires. First on the list was, "car."

As the couple discussed their desire, the conversation turned to the gentleman's talent as a mechanic. This convinced the couple to set their sights on an inexpensive second-hand car.

It was at this point that a woman seated next to them stood up and interrupted their conversation. The woman was in a rush, and said to the couple, "Listen, I don't mean to seem rude, but I've just realized that I've come to the wrong restaurant to meet a friend and so I have to leave." She then handed the couple a set of car keys and added, "I couldn't help overhearing that you're a mechanic. My car is outside. It runs great, but it's older and I don't want to bother with it anymore. I doubt I could get more than a couple thousand dollars for it, but you can probably do something with it. It's yours if you want it."

The energy around us is teaming with potential. To achieve a rich, full life, we need to approach our dreams with a sense of professionalism and expertly channel our natural power of creation to fulfill our desires.

REFLECTIONS ON STEP TWO
DESIRE

The second step in the Practice is to create a clear and detailed image or recording of your desire that you can see or hear every day as many times as possible. The key is to keep your thoughts and emotions concentrated on a specific image and its details so that you direct a steady stream of energy toward it. When energy is projected uninterrupted, it accumulates quickly to a level where it can materialize in the outer world.

As with all the steps in the Practice, Step Two works on many levels. It's here, in the detail and design of your desire, that you forge the conditions of your life. You exercise and expand your imagination. You begin to tap the creative energy within you to experience limitlessness and possibility. You strengthen your will, faith, expectation and love. You dissolve the barriers to your creative power and align yourself more and more with one-pointed pure thought, opening your mind and preparing yourself to receive a greater flow of energy.

Here are some points for reflection. You might like to choose just one point to focus on as a reminder for the day or week. Perhaps write it out and carry it with you.

• Be conscious of what you ask for and accept into your life. The thoughts you hold most often in your mind shape your life. When you say "I can't" or "impossible," you produce a barrier to your creativity and block opportunities from your life. The energy around you stagnates and is rendered ineffective and dissipates. Instead of saying, "I can't," say, "I choose instead..." or "I would prefer...."

If exposed to undesirable conditions, instead of responding negatively, make it a habit to say, "Interesting." Interest arouses feelings of curiosity, which evokes a desire to explore. By saying, "interesting," you detach from the event and project your thoughts into the realm of possibility and learning, where you can exercise your imagination.

• Do you really expect a better life for yourself? Any time you find yourself bewailing the past and thinking about regrets, stop. Use your imagination to live the details of your desire. Enjoy this second of your life. Live in this moment and create the experiences you want, *right now.*

Every moment is a choice, each second can change your life, and all you need is your imagination to create a new and better way, a greater possibility, and a different outlook. What will you imagine? Something small or something grand!

• When you awake in the morning, immediately implant the thought of expectation into your mind. Think and repeat out loud, "I expect…" and state your desire. Review your desire and create an overwhelming feeling of anticipation and excitement. Be eager to start your day. This is an exercise that will eventually become a habit.

• Form a habit of faith in your thoughts and in your life. Ask yourself, "What do I believe? And what more can I choose to believe in the next second?"

• As much as possible throughout the day, build a feeling of love within you and release it into the world outside you. You can do this standing at a bus stop, while you eat your lunch or wait for the photocopier to finish.

Focus on your desire and think about the energy all around you working in every moment to bring you your desires. Create a sense of love and appreciation for what is being created and project your love to others.

• Whenever possible, sit down and write out (or record) detail about your desire. (Remember, use this exercise as a tool to expand your thinking and replace negative thinking with clear, focused thoughts and positive emotions.)

Throughout the day, imagine and enjoy the details of your desire and start conditioning your mind to have a definite purpose and dynamic energy at all times. You will soon discover that even your wandering thoughts are aligned with your goals.

• At night, when you lay down to sleep, review the details of your desire in your mind. Program your thoughts with a series of specific images about your desire. You will soon find yourself reflecting these thoughts in your sleep. You may be surprised to awaken to ideas and innovations you never dreamed possible in your daily thoughts.

• Imagine this: we might fly to the moon one day! What do you say to this? And what would you have said to this just a few decades ago? What would you say now to someone suggesting that we might live on other planets one day? Can we grow back an arm or a leg? Repair a spinal cord? You will likely say, give us ten years, tops! It is said that creation is only ever ten years behind imagination.

Expand your imagination. Leonardo da Vinci wrote, on his design of the world's first airplane, "There shall be wings."

Give your imagination wings and concentrate your mind daily on building bigger mental concepts. Use the detail of your desire to expand your will, faith, expectation and love. Make it your goal to find a solution in everything. Find the possibility. See how everything can be made new or different.

• Throughout the day, think about what you believe, expect and love and mentally complete the following sentences: "I believe…" "I expect…" "I love…" For example, you might think, "I believe I am a success. I expect things to come to me easily. I love what I'm doing. I love my health." You can focus on your desire if you like, but also think broadly and expansively and consider all the areas of your life.

Remember, the energy around you responds to what you project most often. Thus, you may not be living the life you want now, but know with absolute certainty that you are orchestrating the conditions of your life with each thought.

For example, I was having a cup of tea one afternoon and thinking about getting a filing cabinet. I pictured a black, two-drawer, lockable cabinet. I remember thinking, "I'll get this. I expect it will be easy to find." An hour later I felt urged to go for a drive. Three times I picked up my car keys and set them down—I didn't have anywhere to go. However, the feeling wouldn't leave me so I finally decided to go to my car. I left my apartment, got into the elevator and headed down to the parking lot. When the elevator doors opened, there, right outside the elevator was a black, two-drawer, lockable filing cabinet complete with hanging files and a note that read, "Help yourself."

• Carry this phrase with you: *when you feel little, think big!* Any time you feel constrained by others, your own fears and limitations, think big!

Consider this: quite often 90 percent of the upset we have in our lives—the fears, worries, anger or pain—is caused by less than 1 percent of our experiences. From the one thing that happened—the single embarrassing moment or troublesome event, the one time no one liked us—we accept a lifetime of anguish.

Rather than spend our life battling the first twelve years of living or that one experience, we must use our imagination to go beyond these experiences. The more expansive your thoughts, the more expansive your reality. "When you feel little, think big!"

• There are no idle thoughts. Every thought is pregnant with the possibility to create!

It may help you to stay alert and monitor the content of your thoughts if you imagine your thoughts and energy as color. All around you is a sparkling of color, thousands of tiny glittering fireworks. Some thoughts are weak and dissipate. Others are met with opposition by your own chaotic thinking and effectively cancelled out, while clear, intense, desirous thoughts release an enormous burst of light and color that shoots up and out at great distances.

Concentrate on releasing a fireworks display of continually erupting positive energy. Project strong clear images of desire and charge your energy with dynamic emotions. See it with your imagination to appreciate what you are accomplishing each time you make the effort to review the details of your desire and practice a single, positive pattern of thought.

You will experience remarkable benefits instantly. When you mentally experience a desirable event, the physiology of your body responds in kind. Think about your desire and when you return from your reverie you will likely find yourself smiling, feeling warm, energized and secure.

trueprint

You cannot abandon what you do not know.
To go beyond yourself, you must know yourself.
—Sri Nisargadatta Maharaj

I am everything I need to be and
everything I need is in me

PRINCIPLES
DIVINE INTELLIGENCE

At this point, you have set the stage to continuously experience the flow of higher-level energy in your life, an experience often described as "going with the flow" or "connecting with your higher self or mind."

Your third step is the practical means to *go with the flow*, to cultivate your connection to the higher-level energy of creation and more and more attune yourself with its infinite rewards and *flow*.

However, this is a flow of power that we have yet to fully appreciate. And at this stage in our journey, if we are to fully connect with energy at this level, we need to go beyond the simple definition of energy as a force or power and appreciate energy as a *living* force and power.

Therefore, this next section will introduce you to what is perhaps the most intriguing of all the principles we'll look at together, the *Principle of Divine Intelligence*. It reveals the true power of energy, that of infinite intelligence and consciousness.

By the time you finish reading through the following principles, you will understand the flow of energy between you and all things as a flow of communication. This will tie together everything we've talked about so far and bring you to clearly know how it is that you can so easily attract, direct, organize and evolve the energy that makes up our world.

More importantly, once you understand energy as a flow of communication, you will find yourself in a position to recognize how it manifests in your life, as a very personal and powerful language—the language of your soul, which you can invoke to tune into the energy of your higher mind, so that you may continuously experience the flow of divine wisdom and the potent and abundant power in your life.

The Principle of Divine Intelligence

Metaphysics has long described energy as organic, which means that it has the characteristics of a living organism, that of consciousness or *intelligence.*

Scientists encountered the organic nature of energy years ago while working with particles of light, which Einstein called photons. In effect, what the scientists were doing was firing these individual photons, like shooting bullets from a gun. And they assumed, quite logically, that they would be able to aim the "gun" and watch the particles go where directed.

As it turned out, the particles of light didn't perform as anticipated. Indeed, they seemed to be making choices about where to go—educated choices. It appeared as though the results of previous experiments with light energy had somehow been communicated to all particles of light. Each time the scientists worked with a completely new particle, it seemed to already know the results of earlier tests and used the information to make choices about what it would do.

This would be like you writing a test and all other human beings knowing the answers as soon as you finished!

Of course, knowing all the answers is useful only if you know what question is being asked. So the puzzle is this: how could particles of light know what question was being asked? Never mind that—how could particles of light even know what a question is? And to confuse matters further, the scientists weren't asking the same question every time. They were controlling one of two variables—in other words, they were changing the test questions! Yet, the particles of light seemed to know what the experimenters were doing and acted accordingly.

Again, let me put this into perspective. Assume I conduct a test as follows: I write two test questions on a piece of paper. Then I select one of the questions to ask you, except I don't tell you the question and I don't show you the paper. (And if you're a particle of light, how can I?) Now, how can you possibly answer the question, never mind correctly? Yet, the particles of light seemed to do just this—answer correctly. Energy performed as a thinking being. It appeared to be in communication with other energy, aware of past events and everything happening around it, and conscious of, well, everything!

Here is the organic nature of energy and a startling conclusion for scientists: energy has consciousness, which is awareness of one's self and surroundings. Energy has intelligence. It appears to process information and *instantly* share the information with other particles of energy. And it does so in an intimate and immediate way, without sound or words or, seemingly, signals of any kind.

The experiment described for you here is reflective of many, including the Einstein-Podolsky-Rosen (EPR) experiment. In the EPR experiment, two particles were sent flying in opposite directions. Then, in mid-flight, scientists changed one of the particles. Instantly, the other particle, though far away, knew this and changed itself accordingly.

For spiritualists, this phenomenon is a centuries-old understanding. All energy is connected! What happens to some energy ultimately affects all. Energy is a *living* life force, a web of conscious entities communicating at a speed faster than light.

Interestingly, the language of metaphysics and science are growing ever closer together. Nonetheless, science is quantifying and describing a truth that can be readily and immediately experienced otherwise. We can attune ourselves to the energy within and around us and experience the same intimate and instantaneous flow of communication.

Indeed, we're bringing ourselves through this Practice, particularly now in Step Three, to receive, listen and respond to the information that flows back to us. We want to impart our wishes and also receive the flow of divine intelligence that will lead us to create in ever more abundant and miraculous ways.

ENERGY AS COMMUNICATION

Knowing that energy is organic and shares intimate and instantaneous communication, you can clearly see how it is that you are able to so easily *attract, direct, organize* and *evolve* energy. Each principle is an effect of this vast invisible network of communication.

Attraction, for example, describes our ability to communicate with energy at different levels. Direction describes our ability to focus our communication and "speak" to a particular representation of energy at a given level, such as a specific person or thing. Organization and evolution describe the content of the conversation and the reciprocal or two-way nature of our communication with energy.

In other words, attraction is not just describing a force whereby we experience more or less energy at a higher or lower vibration or quality. Rather, attraction describes our ability to receive and impart information with energy at a given level. Of course, how we control our thoughts determines the level or quality of communication we experience.

Thus, our thoughts instantly connect us, quite literally, with like-minded energy. And, as we know, we can elevate our thoughts and connect with the subtle field of creative energy within us, the basic creative energy within all things, thereby transmitting our intentions to a vast intelligence. This is energy that is quick to respond and easily transformed. We can then organize the energy accordingly and mould, shape and change our physical surroundings. We can do so easily.

For example, I recall a study in which scientists prepared two petri dishes with live cells, into which they intended to inject invading bacteria. However, just before they did, the scientists asked a group of people, accustomed to prayer, to form a circle around the second dish and concentrate on preventing the bacteria from invading the culture. In the first dish, the bacteria quickly infected the original cells. However, in the second dish, the bacteria were unable to penetrate the culture and could be seen clustered around the rim of the dish.

> We can talk to the *energy* of people and things easier than we can talk to people and things.

For emphasis, let me say again, we can talk to the *energy* of people and things easier than we can talk to people and things. There are no barriers to energy. Energy is not blocked or limited by physical structures, walls or distance. Your thoughts can instantly travel the globe and communicate with energy, as you choose.

You can direct or, more accurately, communicate your thoughts to a specific person, event or object just as you can call out someone's name in a crowd of people and instantly connect. You can direct or "ask" energy to search out the things you want or direct energy inward and relay instructions of healing and transformation to your body and produce instantaneous and miraculous changes.

An example of this is a video study that detailed the lives of two women. The first woman appeared witty, lively and well groomed. After she spoke for some time, the interviewer introduced a second woman. She was older than the first, had visibly deep lines in her face, appeared unhappy and spoke with a sullen, raspy voice.

Then, suddenly, in the same chair, in the same clothes, there appeared the first woman again. As if by some magical materialization, woman number one was now sitting in the chair smiling.

It turned out that these women were *one in the same.* This young-and-old lady had multiple personality disorder. What was truly startling was the fact that the woman's first personality was healthy as a horse, not a thing wrong with her. Yet, her second personality was seriously diabetic, to the point of requiring regular medication.

> Much like a fish in water, we are immersed in a great sea of energy, an incredible substance that "listens" and responds to us.

It bears repeating: we can communicate with the energy within and around us and produce miraculous change. Energy is a vast intelligence. We live and move in an incredible substance that "listens" and responds to bring us the experiences we need and want to have and that ultimately move us to a greater understanding.

THE GREAT SEA OF ENERGY

This is the *great sea of energy* in which you live and have your being. You are immersed in a Divine Intelligence, God, Goddess, Spirit, Essence or Source. It is an intelligence that fills the universe and exists in even the tiniest energized forms. And as energy evolves and can never die, it is an intelligence that houses the collective consciousness of countless generations.

You exist as a unique expression of energy, an extension of this divine consciousness. Within you is the same creative consciousness from which you were created and that you can, in turn, extend to create all things you imagine.

YOUR DIVINE CENTER OF CONSCIOUSNESS

Your divine center of consciousness is your higher mind or self. This is your creative center, essence or soul that we talked about in Step Two. It's the subtle field of energy and *intelligence* that is the very heart of who you are. It is your higher aspect, your divinity. It is the divine intelligence manifest within you.

Your higher consciousness is at all times connected to the pure consciousness that fills the universe. There is a constant flow of energy between your higher mind and the divine mind, connecting you with a source of infinite wisdom and power and infusing your creations with pure energy and intelligence.

When you are connected with your higher mind, you receive guidance and experience ideas, innovations and inspiration that can cause you to create in new and beautiful ways.

When you are connected with your higher mind, your natural state is characterized by a sense of assurance, security, peace, happiness and fulfillment. Connecting with your higher mind gives you an experience of knowing or immediate understanding without conscious reasoning. You come to know and experience yourself as whole and complete. You experience your inner truth and know yourself as the true creative force you are.

When you are connected with your higher mind or self, you express yourself genuinely. You realize your natural and unique gifts. You begin to think and do the things you love, things that fill you with excitement and joy, and you share your unique expression of divinity with others. This is your higher purpose, to be as you are.

We often experience this connection, *being* as our higher self, when we give to others freely or fall in love. It is a feeling of being on top of the world, where everything seems right and we feel as if we could move mountains.

CONNECTING TO YOUR HIGHER SELF

You can easily reach your higher mind when you tune in to its frequency. It's like listening to a radio. You have to be tuned in to the right station if you want to receive a particular broadcast.

When you want to reach your divine center, you need to tune in to your own spiritual communication, which reflects the flow of communication between your higher mind and the Divine Intelligence. This is the language of your soul.

THE LANGUAGE OF YOUR SOUL

The spiritual language of your soul is how the flow of higher energy manifests to you. It is words, ideas and images that express and call forth the positive, uplifting, energizing and healing qualities of your higher mind. The language of your soul describes your higher mind or consciousness in the particular and personal language that resonates with your soul and evokes a cascade of positive mental, emotional and physical reactions.

You can experience the power of language to uplift and energize, even now, with any generally positive language. For example, state out loud, in a clear voice and with conviction, each of the words in the left-hand column. When you finish, state out loud each of the words in the right-hand column and compare your reactions:

Good	Evil
Beauty	Fear
Happy	Hate
Confidence	Death
Health	Sickness
Youth	Age
Love	Anger
Peace	War
Joy	Pain

The words, images and ideas that fill your consciousness change your breathing, the amount of oxygen you take in and the chemicals released in your body and they lower or raise the vibratory rate of your energy.

Here is a similar example that you can try with another person (and it is an excellent tool for teaching children the important of positive self-talk):

Ask the other person to stand in front of you and raise one arm out to their side at shoulder height. Tell them you will push down on their arm in an attempt to lower it to their side and that they should resist.

However, before you do, tell them to look into your eyes throughout the exercise and repeat this phrase as you push down on their arm: "I am a bad person, I am a really bad person, I am a bad person...."

Now repeat the same exercise, but this time ask the other person to look into your eyes and repeat the following phrase as you apply pressure to their arm: "I am a great person. I am a really great person, I am a great person...."

You will find that it is very easy to push the other person's arm down when they state negative words. On the other hand, it is near impossible to lower their arm when they are making positive statements.

By keeping even a generally positive inner dialogue, you fill yourself with energy and connect more closely with your higher self. But when you take a step further and define the specific language of your soul, you fuse with a higher vibration and experience currents of divine energy flowing through you, mind, body and soul.

TRUEPRINT:
MAPPING THE LANGUAGE OF YOUR SOUL

A Trueprint maps the language of your soul and gives you the words and imagery to connect with your divinity and tap into the vast sea of intelligence whenever you like.

"True" refers here to that which reflects your essential and genuine character. What is "true" is your divinity, the higher aspect within you, wherein the divine intelligence is manifest.

The word *print* means to impress on the mind or memory. It is the mark or impression made by one body on another.

Your consciousness has been imprinted with your divinity. It also carries the marks left by experience and fear. A Trueprint guides you to systematically sort through impressions and marks on your consciousness to reveal your higher truths, the inspiring, healing and energizing images and ideas reflective of your divinity.

Thus, a Trueprint is bringing forth your divinity, making it tangible through words. In other words, it's creating a "print" or reproduction or your "truth."

A Trueprint provides you with a map to journey through your awareness and discover what you hold to be true about yourself, what you choose, believe, expect and love for yourself. It will guide you to peel away layers of perception that have built up over the years, to uncover those truths that reflect your perfect, whole and complete self.

This is a meditative time where you can reproduce your truth in a language that you understand. And because *you* define the language of your soul and the meaning of the words, you will be better able to form a commitment to the definitions you choose.

Your Trueprint, then, will become a commitment to live from your higher self. It will become a filter for your perception. It will guide your thoughts, feelings and actions.

Simply, your Trueprint will give you a personal talisman, a key you carry with you that will exert power and influence in your life. This key is a concrete representation of your divinity, a tangible expression of your soul that you can actively imprint on the world. In so doing, you will come to continually experience the flow of divine energy.

Your Trueprint will serve as a tool you can use to replace mental clutter. Instead of exercising anger, fear or hurt, you can exercise the qualities of your soul. Instead of tearing down your creations throughout the day with destructive thoughts and actions, you can fuel your creations with the dynamic qualities of your soul.

Each time you practice this form of spiritual communication with the divine center of your consciousness, you build the connection to your higher self, like exercising a muscle. Each time you raise your consciousness and attune your thoughts with the ideas and images reflective of your higher mind, you strengthen your connection. Very quickly, you will find that you can reach in to the center of your soul whenever you like and draw upon an infinite source of energy and wisdom. Whenever you need, you can return to the commitment you create here and receive the guidance and wisdom of your higher mind.

Now Is the Time to Create a Bridge to Your Higher Mind

Perhaps, at times you've prayed or meditated and your experiences were less than you hoped. This is true for many of us, and for all the reasons discussed so far. It's difficult to experience our connection to a higher flow of communication when our energy is low or we seek to do so all of a sudden, "out of the blue." It's easy to do so if we elevate our energy little by little and familiarize ourselves with a higher flow so that we can maintain it. And it's important to expose ourselves to more expansive thoughts, images and feelings so that we can recognize the manifestation of a higher flow of energy in our life.

You have accomplished all of this. You have brought two simple steps into your life, but in fact you have accomplished so much more. You've elevated your energy more and more, first through mental clearing, then again through physical clearing, and again through detailing. You've already begun to tap into the subtle energy at the heart of you by releasing the dynamic emotions of your higher mind through the creative expression of your desires. You've removed layer after layer of stagnant energy smothering your divinity and clouding your perception. You have established one-pointed thought, aligning your energy with the pure consciousness that fills the universe.

Now is the appropriate time to create a bridge to your higher mind. You've acclimatized yourself to journey to the higher regions of consciousness.

Let me invite you to experience the spiritual language of your higher mind—a language you can use to invoke a state of consciousness that will allow you to channel the wisdom and power of the *Divine Intelligence.* And you will be amazed how just spending time thinking about your higher awareness at this point fills you with energy and warmth.

METHOD
MAPPING THE LANGUAGE OF YOUR SOUL

To begin, set aside some time when you won't be disturbed. You can spend as much time as you like with this exercise. You may even wish to come back to it a few times over the next little while to make small refinements or just enjoy being immersed in thinking about your higher qualities.

You will need a pen and paper or a recording device and you may want to put on some soothing music, light some candles or dim the lights (only slightly as you will need light to write). Make sure that you're comfortable and relaxed. Give yourself time to enjoy an almost meditative state immersed in your own awareness. (If someone is assisting you, make sure you feel comfortable working with this person.)

I AM

At the top of a sheet of paper, write the words, "I AM." Make a list of all the words, ideas, images, feelings or even stories that reflect what you have accepted as representing a truth about yourself. This is a list that contains both positive and negative descriptors. For example, "I am giving" or "I am a worrier."

The words you choose only have to work for you. You do not have to choose descriptors that would make sense to someone else. I have seen words like "mellow" and "warm" chosen to represent a whole host of actions, qualities and feelings that I would never have thought to associate with these words. If a word makes sense to you and describes a truth about you, then that's all that matters. You are endeavoring to describe the indescribable—the language of your soul.

List everything that you believe and have accepted as representing a truth about yourself, at one time or another, briefly or enduringly, willingly or begrudgingly. Consider all that you have been and that still endures, for better or worse. Consider all that you are now and all you could be in the future.

Everything you have accepted as truth about yourself has touched your mind and left a mark that, in some way, great or small, has shaped your pattern of thought, affecting your will, faith, expectation, acceptance and love. These beliefs can either hide or reveal, block or connect you with your perfect, whole and complete higher self.

I have seen lists that take up many pages and ones that barely fill half a page. Your list may look something like the one that follows.

I am honest, a liar, happy, sad, ugly, beautiful, mean, generous, good, loving, guilt ridden, fearful, in pain, open-minded, faithful, defensive, defenceless, trusting, suspicious, argumentative, pleasing, tolerant, busy, lazy, physical, mental, a dreamer, a pragmatist, kind, hurtful, rude, accepting, full of anxiety, nervous, worried, afraid, hopeful, unsure, confident, murderous, self-sacrificing, good, bad, simple, complicated, confused, indifferent, solid, weak, strong, secretive, sick, skinny, fat, cowardly, warm, content, lazy, addictive, funny, stingy, bold, a floozy, vivacious, mad, sincere, playful, tender, a perfectionist, thankful....

This is a list of your inner truths, as applied by you or *others*. It doesn't matter to what degree you have accepted these truths. It is a list of all that you believe is possible about yourself, all that you can be and might be in the future.

To help you create your list, consider some of the following points:

PROTEST: Look at words, or more accurately, the *meaning* attached to words that evoke in you a strong negative response. These are qualities that strike a chord with you—thoughts, feelings, ideas or actions that irritate, anger or upset you. Simply, consider descriptors that you feel *don't* apply to you and cause you to *react* strongly. Ask yourself, "Are there any words or ideas that, when others use them to describe me, I feel uncomfortable?"

Often, the qualities we fight against most strongly hold meaning for us. Somewhere deep down, there is a measure of truth in these words. For example, I may have listened to others comment that I am ugly and, to a degree, felt unpleasant. The word "ugly" bothered me, and so there exists of measure of truth in this word for me. If I truly believe that I am beautiful, all the time, then such a word, or one of a similar meaning, would have no impact on my consciousness. It wouldn't bother me because I would have no attachment, faith or belief in this word.

If there are words that you adamantly refuse to list because they elicit feelings of defensiveness—for example, "critical" or "mean"—then consider if perhaps you fear these words and their implications. Perhaps there is a part of you that believes it possible for you to be "critical" or "mean," and you want so strongly for this not to be true that you are fighting against it.

Consider listing any words that evoke a strong reaction.

PROJECT: Consider looking at any words that you regularly assign to others. For example, do you tend to label others as "weak" and repeatedly use this word?

What we project onto others very often has meaning and importance for us. If I say that someone is weak, I may inwardly fear weakness. I want so badly to be seen as strong that I notice any sign of weakness outside myself. Take a moment to rummage in your memory and see if there are any negative descriptive words that you tend to project onto others, such as wimp, jerk, mean, flighty, stressed.

We also tend to project qualities onto others when we feel something is lacking in our lives. So, we project onto others what we desperately want to have. For example, we may be feeling sad and want so badly to be happy that we start noticing every happy person. Suddenly it seems as if the whole world is happy but us. And so, we might say regularly, "How come others always seem to be so happy," or "She is so happy." Consider any positive words you regularly use to label others: happy, energetic, full of life, powerful, warm, sincere, content, secure, together.

When you feel that you have exhausted all the truths you strongly believe reflect your consciousness, considering past and present as well as future capabilities, apply the next variable: *Choice.*

CHOICE

"*Choice*" for our purposes has a very limited definition. Ask yourself, what do I choose to give and receive *all the time*, from *all* persons. Thus, the second variable, choice, is directing you to choose those qualities that you want to give and receive at all times.

Go through your list and circle the words that you feel fit with the definition of *choice*.

Now let me add an important point. You are taking a moment, not long, to really sit with your negative and positive choices and allow them to simply exist on paper, outside of yourself. It is an exercise in seeing truth and choice. Each characteristic, quality or feeling is a word, or series of words, laid out before you awaiting a choice. This is all they are: words, lines, symbols on the paper.

It should become evident that nothing has any meaning except that which you assign to it. You can choose the definitions and, so doing, choose who you are and what the world is like that you live in. You can choose who you are now, on paper, just as you do in every moment. Your every thought and emotion is a choice. A conscious and productive choice is one that comes from an awareness of who you are now, who you truly are and who you choose to be.

In other words, no one can make us be, or not be, anything. For example, you are enjoying a quiet moment right now, but suppose that, in a minute, someone starts yelling at you. In this minute, you haven't changed. You haven't suddenly lost your ability to choose. You are left with the same choices you have now. When the disturbance happens, you can choose to be true to your higher self, as you can choose now, or you can choose to let someone else choose for you and take on his or her anger.

You are making the same choices in this moment that you are faced with in every moment.

Take some time to consider the meaning, imagery and energy of the words you choose. Spend some time writing out corresponding descriptions. This can be brief or involved. It is a useful exercise, however, and other words may come to mind.

Consider some of the following questions to help you select and define the words that will represent what you choose to give and receive all the time:

1. What does this word mean in terms of my thoughts, feelings and actions?

2. How will I express this quality in thought, feeling and action?

3. How do others express this quality? How will I recognize when someone is giving this quality to me?

4. How will I know when I'm giving this quality?

5. How will I give this quality in each moment, each second? What does this look like? Is this something I hold in my thoughts alone?

As you continue to define the words you select, creating images, actions and associated feelings for each word, consider the following.

There are numerous courses that encourage us to live by our higher ideals and truths, core beliefs, or what are sometimes called foundational principles—the principles that guide our thoughts, feelings and actions. Such descriptors form the core of our perception. They connect us with the world and our higher self. Often, though, we're left to wonder what these principles might be.

More often, however, we're told what these principles *should* be. We're presented with a list of words like trust, love or abundance. Such words certainly appear to represent some sort of universal goodness. Who wouldn't nod their head and agree to such words? Eventually, though, we might realize that we have accepted these words, without spending the time to consider what they mean to us or how we're going to carry out these principles minute to minute.

Take the word "trust" for instance. Think of how many associations you have to this word. What springs to mind when you think of trust? Is this something you earn over the long run? Can you trust minute by minute? And how do you do that? What does trust look like? How do you go about your life in a state of trust? When someone's yelling at you or you feel that you've messed up or been wronged, what do you do in that minute that's trusting? When you're hurt, how do you trust or forgive? Do you forgive because you trust? What should you be doing, in this moment, to live your life according to trust? How do you receive trust? Is this inner quality something that you give away, or do you give it to yourself?

Only you can define the specific guiding principles of your unique soul.

You should absolutely know the particular truths that connect you with your higher self and form the foundation of your life. Knowing these truths, you can practice a spiritual communication minute to minute, in thought, emotion and action. *But only you can do this!* No one else can define the language of your soul.

Thus, rather than simply accepting qualities from a general one-size-fits-all word list to which you have no personal relationship, you are creating your Trueprint by defining the specific guiding principles of your unique soul.

Spend some time thinking about the meaning of the words you choose. State the word in your mind and out loud. Close your eyes and feel the word. Does it have color? Sound? Imagine yourself living this quality in each moment and picture how you think, feel and act as you give and receive this quality. Give your higher mind a moment to speak to you.

The words you select using the definition of *choice* (that which you choose to give and receive *all the time*) are creative commands tailor-made to reach your higher consciousness. They are words that reflect the positive energy of your Divine Mind and fill you with warmth or give you a jolt of positive energy as you think and speak them. These words fill your mind and heart with peace, assurance, confidence and security. They are words that bring out the best in you.

As you continue to select the language of your soul, you will quickly notice that many of the words we so readily consider important might not work with our definition of *choice*. Take beauty, for example: "I choose to give beauty all the time and I choose to receive beauty all the time, from everyone and all things."

How will I give beauty and what does it mean to receive beauty? If the definition of beauty is related solely to physical appearance, it likely doesn't make sense according to the definition of *choice*. And yet, much of the time, we assign great meaning to physical appearance. If beauty is a word that, for you, means all that is gracious, kind and forgiving in the world, and you wish to give and receive this sense of beauty all the time, then this is a word that has great meaning for you and applies.

You may have chosen words like smart or imaginative. If, by your definition, it is important to you to give this sense of smartness and imagination to everyone all of the time, and to receive, in return, smart and imaginative gifts, then keep this word. It is not a question of whether or not you feel others will give you this all the time; it is what you want to be possible. These descriptors are the guiding principles of your life, the qualities of your soul that you wish to imprint on the events, actions, and objects around you, all of the time.

Eliminate any qualities that simply don't make sense to you or fit with the definition of *choice*. You may also decide to disregard certain words, because they are simply not the most important words to you.

For example, I listed the word, "strong," but as I began to define it, I decided it didn't reflect what I most wanted to give and receive all the time. More importantly, I didn't feel that this word and its meaning returned any benefit of real importance to me. I didn't feel that it had any bearing on my soul. As I imagined living this quality every day, it simply didn't fill me with a sense of creative power and energy.

Remember, you are not limited here by a sense of reality. You are describing the perfection of your soul, both as you experience it and want it to be.

For example, someone might suggest that they feel it's important to shed tears some of the time and will want to keep a word like sad, which could mean to them an experience of pity or an overwhelming feeling. Keep in mind that we are describing our best life and what we want to give and receive *all of the time*, not just some of the time.

There are likely words or ideals that you will condense into one word that incorporates several qualities. One woman chose the word love to mean, among other things, warmth, trust, truth, generosity, kindness, caring, openness, and passion—one word to express an experience of shared and overwhelming joy. It may be difficult for anyone else to understand this full description of thought and action, but if a word makes sense to you and keeps you conscious of the higher qualities of your soul, then it is likely the best word to use.

Your list may now look something like the one that follows. This was part of my initial list. The words crossed out represent either those that simply did not make sense to me according to the definition of *choice* or ones that I felt were already incorporated into other meanings.

~~Solid~~	Loving
~~Promising~~	~~Ugly~~
~~Innocent~~	~~Active~~
Creative	~~Punctual~~
~~Aggressive~~	~~Passive~~
~~Independent~~	~~Achiever~~
~~Hopeful~~	~~Aloof~~

Peacefulness	~~Prudent~~
Intelligent	~~Modest~~
~~Carefree~~	~~Greedy~~
~~Committed~~	Trustworthy
~~Initiative~~	~~Angry~~
~~Persistence~~	~~Mean~~
~~Brave~~	~~Committing~~
Generous	~~Free~~
True	~~Determined~~
~~Honest~~	Present
Joy	~~Worrier~~
~~Idealistic~~	~~Strong~~

My final list included the words shown here, and a few more I thought to add:

Defencelessness

Faithful

Courageous

Review the words you have selected against the narrow definition of choice—*that which I wish to give and receive all the time, from all persons*—and when you feel satisfied with the words and definitions you've chosen, move on to the next variable.

VALUE

The next variable to apply is *value.* Using the definition that follows, select the words you feel are most "valuable" from your revised list.

Value is an abstract concept of what is right, desirable, worthy and important. What is "valuable" to the soul are qualities that increase in worth and importance as you give them away. *Value is that which increases by the giving of it.* Let me explain.

You cannot give what you don't have. If you want to give happiness to someone, you must first have happiness yourself. Therefore, when you give happiness, you instantly prove that you have something. In fact, you end up with more in the instant that you give it away.

In the moment that you share a laugh or a smile, you witness that you are happy. You experience it and more fully than before. Your happiness grows from an intellectualized concept to a physical, emotional and spiritual truth. Moreover, you prove that you believe happiness is desirable and important for you and others. You increase and strengthen what you will, believe, expect and love for yourself and others. You enhance your own sense of happiness and its value to you. By giving happiness away, you gain a sense of who you are.

And of course, when you give happiness, it is now for someone else. And what you give is likely to be reciprocated and shared, such that happiness increases even more.

Value, then, is that which gains worth, importance and desirability by the giving of it.

Thus, when you give the qualities of value that you now choose, you teach yourself who you are. And the more you give

What do I want to give myself? | of your true self, the more you learn of your divinity. And soon, you learn the lesson your higher self is teaching you and you become as you are.

You could say that every quality that remains on your list is *valuable*. Each remaining quality will increase as you give it away. Yes, every quality will teach you who you are as you give it away. So, take time now to sit with each word that remains on your list and ask yourself:

"What do I most want to give myself?"
"What do I most want to teach myself in each moment?"
"What qualities do I most want to accept, believe, expect and love about myself?"

Let me also remind you here that energy is a web of relationships. What you give to *yourself* you also contribute to all. Even when you think about *valuable* qualities in private, you extend them to all, for they color your energy, which is connected to all things.

So you have to ask yourself, "Do I wish to contribute this quality I now choose to everyone? Is this what I would give and cause to increase beyond myself?

Know, also, that the qualities you now select not only teach you who you are, they also teach others how to treat you. The qualities you accept and deeply believe about yourself come through in your body language, your words and actions. Others pick up on your "inner truths" and treat you accordingly. You cannot hide what you really believe about yourself. You exude your truths through your skin. Thus, the qualities you give yourself will always be returned to you by others and through the conditions of your life.

This is an important point. Let me share with you a story that illustrates the importance of taking care of what you give yourself, first and foremost, in thought.

For ten years, Myra got up every day and forced herself to work at a job she absolutely hated. She kept telling herself she earned a decent living and should just keep going, save money, and do the best she could.

She was always hoping and wishing for something better, or so she thought. But the truth is, deep down, she expected and believed tha' she would struggle. She expected to pay for everything she got w'

We so often hope for more when all we really think about is less.

blood, sweat and tears. It's all she thought about—how every day would be hard and she would always be exhausted. She expected others to treat her poorly and was convinced that no one appreciated what she did.

Her every thought and action screamed out her terror and fears—fear of not having enough money, security or a career down the road. She worked every day to save for tomorrow. She counted the minutes and passed the time with thoughts of "maybe one day."

So you see, Myra said she wanted more, but all she really *thought* about was less. And she was getting exactly what she desired—she believed and expected less and that is exactly what she lived, every day.

One morning, Myra sat down with a pen and paper and made a list of exactly what she would give herself. Within that week, a company she admired created a new position that just happened to perfectly match her ideal job in title and description. She was offered the job and at the exact salary she wanted.

Interestingly, her current employer offered to increase her salary and give her time off with pay to reconsider and rest. This was the same employer who before had never offered her a simple "thank you."

The moment Myra changed what she was willing to give herself, she instantly changed how others treated her.

Take time to review each word that remains on your list and select the words you decide are *valuable*. Choose the qualities and feelings that you most want to give yourself and increase and share in every moment.

In truth, you will intuitively recognize your most valuable qualities. Just as there are thoughts that form barriers, like closed doors, shutting you off from the flow of Divine Intelligence, there are also words, images, ideas and feelings that serve as keys unlocking your particular doors—images and feelings that instantly open you to a higher flow of energy, wisdom and power and return you to your greater truth.

YOUR FINAL WORD LIST

In creating your final words, it is best to select a short list that you can easily repeat to yourself and, in an instant, deliver. I recommend three words. This is your trinity.

When you have chosen the trinity that will form the final print of your inner truth, clearly write out each word on a piece of paper. Take a moment to repeat each word. These qualities, feelings and images are the language of your soul and the filter through which you will now see the world.

My final word list included:

Love
Defencelessness
Joy

I felt that, of all the qualities that remained on my list, these words represented what I most want to teach myself and increase within me. These are the qualities I want to extend and witness. These qualities are what I *will, believe, accept* and want most to *expect* for myself.

I chose *love* to represent an openness that cannot be described by words. I see it in my mind as though I am opening up my entire being. Just thinking, "love," and seeing its mental image, tells me instantly how to be—that I should open myself up to others. When I think of this quality as my truth, it brings to mind a host of words and experiences in a flash. It evokes a cascade of positive emotions. This word works for me. It tells me exactly what to give and expect from the world. This is one word that I have spent the time to consider and question, and it now forms my core pattern of thought.

I chose *defencelessness* to mean a conscious decision to honor the perfection of my soul. If I am defenceless then there is nothing within me that can be attacked. If I am defensive, then I believe that there is some part of me that requires protection and a part I must attack in others to keep my truth safe. I want instead to be reminded, and to demonstrate, that there is nothing within me that can be attacked, hurt or destroyed. There is nothing lacking, limited or less. If I find myself in a situation where I am allowing myself to become angry or feel any inkling of protectiveness or pain, I simply repeat my commitment to be defenceless.

I chose the word *joy* to represent the exciting experience of anticipation. It is a sense of expectation. For me, this word represents peace, security and happiness, all in one word. I relabel any irritation or upset as expectation and elicit joy in myself. I keep this word as a reminder of my faith in my power to create, knowing that I can expect everything. I want at all times to extend and receive this sense of joy.

This is the map of my soul that I have determined to govern my being, my thoughts and my desires. It is a description that I understand. It is the consolidation of my essence.

Forming Your Commitment

Create now, on paper (or in your mind if you are recording your Trueprint), a circle around the inner truths you selected. Draw the circle slowly and deliberately.

This circle forms your commitment. You are, right now, drawing a line in the sand. It says, "Yes, this is the world I live in. This is how I see the world. This is who I am."

I would ask that you now honor yourself and complete your commitment by reading the following and repeating out loud the italicized sections.

I SHALL RESPECT MYSELF. *I shall give myself my truth, the qualities of my higher self, all the time. I will live authentically and **be** as I am, ever present with my soul.*

To honor and respect yourself, you must give back to yourself. Therefore, respect is not something you give to others, though that will occur. It is giving back to yourself the higher energy, wisdom and abundance of your higher self.

I SHALL BE HONEST WITH MYSELF. *I shall consistently "be" according to my truth, all the time and with all people, actions and events.*

To be honest with yourself, you must be consistent—true. If you believe you are entitled to happiness and yet most of the time you allow yourself to express sadness, then you are not being true to yourself. If you desire more, but constantly worry that you will have less, you are not being true and consistent. You are not being honest with yourself.

I SHALL FORGIVE MYSELF. *I shall cease fueling negative emotions, the barriers to my divinity. If I am feeling angry or hurt, I am giving myself anger and pain. I choose instead to give myself my higher qualities, for what I give, I have. I am my perfect, whole and complete higher self.*

You cannot give what you don't have. Thus, forgiveness is not something you give to others; that will naturally occur. Forgiveness is something you foster in yourself, first. It's something you *can* give yourself. Forgiveness is consistently invoking the language, feelings and energy of your divinity. It's essentially conjuring up the "bridge to your higher mind" and crossing over into a much greater flow of energy, wisdom and power.

Whenever you experience a moment of pain, your commitment will provide for forgiveness. If something causes your jaw to tighten and your back teeth to clench, take a moment to give yourself your higher qualities. Connect in that moment with your higher self, a source of infinite wisdom and power. Ask what you want to give yourself in that moment. Will you give yourself pain or truth, anger or the qualities that enrich your life?

I repeat my words of love, defencelessness and joy. I honor my commitment by giving back to myself the qualities of my soul. And when you give to your soul, you give to all. Eventually, even the most intense anger cannot survive.

Jolene had been angry with her mother for over thirty years. She could hardly bring herself to think about her mother. However, after creating her Trueprint, every time Jolene thought about her mother, she repeated and relished the feelings, images and ideas of her trinity. Several weeks later, Jolene called her mother. And to her surprise, she found herself interacting with her mother with the language and actions associated with her Trueprint. Even more surprising to Jolene was that she actually *felt* these words. The anger she had held onto for so long had dissipated.

To give you another example, a gentleman named Roger overheard a good friend put him down in front of a group of his peers. Roger couldn't get over it. He couldn't imagine what he could have done to prompt this. This bit of anger ate at Roger for two years. Meanwhile, the "friend" was completely unbothered. He had been angry about a few things that had been going on in his own life and chose to direct his anger at Roger without thinking. He apologized, but as the friendship was obviously ended, he forgot all about it and went on with his life.

The only one suffering was Roger. But why? In an effort to find out, he went back over his list of "I AM." If the words uttered by his friend were completely untrue, then why was he bothered? Why would he allow a lie to eat at him for two years? Obviously, he must feel that there is a measure of truth in these words.

Roger decided that if the words spoken by his ex-friend were true, they are not true now. If they were untrue, then he was bothered about what others think, which meant that his convictions about himself were on shaky ground. It meant that he didn't love himself and needed others to reinforce what was true about him. He was accepting whatever qualities others assigned to him.

So, Roger repeated back to himself the qualities that he wanted to be, "love, generosity, courage." In that moment, he had a choice between giving these qualities to himself or accepting "anger and feeling little and not so great," as Roger put it.

> Forgiveness, honesty and respect are what you give yourself, first.

Roger lived his higher qualities for a few days, thinking about them, giving them to others and using them to replace negativity. About a week later, he thought about himself and his ex-friend and thought, "how could I give anger to myself and others? How could I close myself off from my own source of power, safety and fulfilment?" Being angry was against every quality in his Trueprint; anger is not generous or courageous. Roger decided that, as he had lived his higher qualities every day, at least positively for the last week, they were all that he was willing to accept about himself. Roger drew a line in the sand and kept his commitment.

After a little more time, Roger noticed that he was no longer angry. In fact, he started to think that if he had been the one to say something so nasty that could only mean he didn't love himself, at least not at that moment. He started to think about the other person and feel for them. Eventually, he consciously extended his thoughts of love, generosity and courage toward his ex-friend.

When you consistently live from your higher qualities, you start to recognize, very quickly, when others are not loving themselves, not accepting and believing and truly feeling something greater and uplifting in their lives. If someone is angry, hurtful or inflicting pain on others, then this is what they are giving, first and foremost, to themselves. You cannot give anger and feel good. You cannot give pain and feel love. We could say that some people might feel a twisted sense of happiness from seeing others suffer, but they cannot feel the overwhelming sense of joy, beauty and peace all wrapped up together that comes from your higher self. You cannot receive the communication of your divinity. You are simply tuned in to the wrong channel.

Your higher self can give you a leap to enlightenment and a feeling and understanding that cannot be described. It's ineffable—too great for words, because it comes from a connection to all things and is infinitely great. Any other high cannot compare.

As with all the steps in this Practice, you don't have to make anything happen. Do the steps, give to yourself and let your higher wisdom lead you and bring you so many amazing gifts. The greatest and most sublime experiences await you.

Applying Your Trueprint

Carry your Trueprint with you. Write it out and carry it in thought. Throughout the day, bring to mind the language of your Trueprint. Superimpose your Trueprint onto every situation, person or thing. Look at others throughout the day and imagine sending the feelings and energy of your Trueprint to them. Express your Trueprint in your thoughts, feelings and actions.

Your Trueprint is a filter through which to see the world. It will guide you in your choices and bring a greater energy, wisdom and power into your life.

Your Trueprint is also a powerful reminder that will direct you toward the path of your higher self and away from the road to negativity. Whenever negativity or upset strikes, or you feel the diminishing of your intent, repeat to yourself one phrase: "What do I want to give myself in this moment?" "What is it going to be?" This is your moment of truth, literally. This is when you decide to be as you truly are or let your thoughts and emotions be controlled by someone or something else.

Certainly, there are a lot of pressures and distractions in the day. It can be challenging to maintain the connection to our higher self. And it's virtually impossible at times to walk away and say, "excuse me, I have to go meditate or visualize," or "just give me a moment, I need to connect with my higher self." You need a quick and immediate key that will bring you back to your inner self and fill your mind with the words and images of your higher source of power.

Your Trueprint is that key. It gives you a second of clarity in which you can make a choice. It gives your emotional muscles the control to flick the metaphorical light switch on and keep it on.

Thus, if someone is yelling at you and you feel your temper rising, ask yourself, "What do I want to give to myself in this moment?" If you are losing faith and struggling to persist, ask the question. If sadness is seeping into your bones, ask yourself the question.

You might pick up the phone and suddenly find yourself in a heated conversation that leaves you shaking. You might run into someone on the street, and the next thing you know, you're exposed to disturbing news. Your boss might offhandedly put you down. You might simply be feeling low from all the pressures and stresses that currently surround you. You might suddenly find yourself embarrassed. In the moment that you feel negativity creeping into your mind, review the words of your Trueprint. State them out loud if you can. Conjure up the images, ideas and feelings you associate with your key words.

Remind yourself that energy has intelligence, and by raising your consciousness to a higher level, you open yourself to receiving guidance, strength and wisdom from this intelligence. Give the energy that flows from a higher source a moment to flow through you and bring you peace and calm.

Remain present with your soul. Stay conscious of your commitment. Be vigilant with your thoughts. Guard your thoughts, and you guard your energy and your destiny.

If you keep your commitment and regularly focus on thinking from your divine center of consciousness, you will soon be able to maintain the feeling of inner power all through the day.

Remember, you do not have to concern yourself with any moment but now. You don't have to concern yourself with how your desire will manifest. You only have to concern yourself with *being* and the universe will manage the rest.

As you work with this exercise over the next little while, you may add or change some of the words you have chosen as you become more aware of your thoughts and continually elevate your energy and open yourself up to a greater flow of energy. Eventually, however, you will reveal the few powerful words that can instantly return you to where you want to be. You will discover which truths have the most power for you, instantly assisting you to keep your commitment. These words will nudge you back to your perfection with a spurt of positive energy.

Each word should immediately fill you, not with a sense of sacrifice, self-righteousness or virtue, but with a sense of pleasure, security and calm. And if you simply take care of you, you automatically take care of us all.

Each step in the Practice gives you a tool to take care of each instant, which is all the time you need to release an abundance of energy and intelligence towards the construction of your desire.

TRUEPRINT AND DESIRE

Your Trueprint will assure that the origins of your desires are of good intent. Purposely selfish and vindictive desires close the channels of creativity and slow the vibratory nature of thought.

We might ask, "are not all desires essentially selfish?" If our desires express our perfect, whole and complete self and bring into our life the conditions that will allow us to operate more freely for the good of all, then the answer, quite simply, is no.

A selfish desire is one that stems from a belief in give-or-take and more-or-less. If I give, then another takes. If I have, then another has less. A soulful desire originates from a belief in abundance. Everyone has the power to create and every creation is a manifestation of the spirit.

Remember, you are an extension of a divine and creative consciousness. You are co-creator of the universe and have dominion over energy for your use. You are entitled to a bountiful life. And you can no more stop creating than you can stop thinking. Creating everything you want in life is simply realizing and manifesting your natural abundant state.

YOUR TRUEPRINT AND YOUR JAILERS

In creating your Trueprint, you may have uncovered some of the strongest negative qualities you struggle against.

Throughout the day, particularly when you feel any form of negativity or distress, notice if you are struggling with any of the negative qualities that remained on your "I AM" list. You may want to add some of the negative descriptors from your Trueprint to your list of *jailers*.

By noticing when any of these triggers pop up, you increase your awareness of your thought process and remind yourself to exercise your Trueprint. As you do, you will soon see yourself moving past many of the fears and upsets listed in your Inventory.

As you give, so shall you receive

As you continue to give to yourself those qualities that connect you with the infinite intelligence, you are building peace and security. And as you do this for yourself, you simultaneously give so much to others, naturally. When you give to yourself your higher qualities and live them, you share a beautiful energy with others. It is enough that you are. Just by entering a room or being near someone else, your energy gives so much. All that you get in return, all the good fortune and things that you manifest, are simply exchange for what you give. "As you give, so shall you receive."

You need do nothing to be deserving of everything. It is enough that you are.

REFLECTIONS ON STEP THREE
TRUEPRINT

Step Three takes you through a gentle meditation to discover the language of your soul. It brings forth words, images and feelings that reflect your higher self and can be used to invoke a higher state of mind and energy. These mental impressions form your Trueprint, a personal talisman you can use to guide your interactions with yourself and others. It is a commitment to consistently respect, be honest with and forgive yourself. The more you exercise your Trueprint, the more you build your connection to your higher self and the higher-level energy in *all that is*.

To assist you in applying your Trueprint, consider the following:

• Throughout the day, fix your mind on the qualities of your Trueprint. Ask yourself, "What am I doing today to express these qualities? What am I thinking or doing today that might be in contradiction to my commitment?"

• Make it a point to outwardly express the qualities of your Trueprint to yourself and others at least once a day. For example, if you chose love as a quality, you might treat yourself to something or spend a dollar more on a great cup of your favorite beverage. You could send a quick and loving note to someone or donate something to charity. If you chose courage, simply choosing to exercise your Trueprint in the face of one of your fears is an excellent way to express this quality. If you chose secure, to mean self-confidence and peace, smile boldly at others, greet them, assist someone and share your talents and knowledge.

• Cultivate the beautiful and powerful qualities of your soul. List and repeat "I AM" statements that reflect the qualities of your higher self and serve as testimony to the power within you. "I AM loving. I AM joyous. I AM capable of creating in the image of my thoughts, extending love and joy."

• Stay conscious with your thoughts. Notice when you are thinking thoughts that return you to an older, less energizing concept of "I AM." Make a point of immediately replacing such thoughts by repeating your commitment. State your trinity out loud or as a mantra in your thoughts.

• You can now add to the detail of your desire all the reasons why this event or object fits with your higher self. Imagine that the universe is sitting next to you and carry out a conversation about your desire and the qualities of your Trueprint.

You may, for example, be thinking about a trip to Hawaii. Concentrate on all the ways in which your desire fits with your commitment of, say, love and joy. You might desire to travel to Hawaii because the harmony of nature so bountifully displayed there evokes in you an immediate expression of *love*. The beauty that surrounds you there reminds you of the growth of your soul. Your desire fills you with *joy* and excitement that extends to all.

> If you want to experience a higher flow, you must begin to think thoughts that echo its characteristics.

visualization

It is possible to imagine something so clearly that,
in time, you can touch it.

In joy, I shout out to creation: this is what I will.
I release my life's design to the abundant universe.
In peace and gratitude, I am silence,
feeling the flow of creation around me,
feeling my purpose lovingly and joyously fulfilled.

PRINCIPLES
CREATION

So far, you've taken steps to control, organize and elevate your thoughts and energy. You've cleared your mind and environment of disruptive mental chatter and unnecessary clutter. You've replaced destructive thoughts with the details of your desire, further expanding and elevating your thoughts with the energizing emotions of will, faith, expectation and love. As well, you've connected to your source by giving and receiving the higher qualities of your true self, gaining access to a higher-level energy that will quickly manifest as your desires.

You've accomplished so much. You've taken small, manageable steps throughout each day to know yourself, your desires and your divinity.

Putting It All Together

Now, it's important to practice applying all the steps together, at the same time, so that thinking effectively, *minute to minute, day to day,* becomes instinctive. Of course, you're likely applying the steps together already; certainly you're applying the steps in quick succession. But by purposefully taking a few minutes each day to focus on combining the steps, you will soon wonder how you could think any other way. And later on, this focused period of practice will give you the opportunity to intensely explore your gifts and experience increasingly greater insights.

Remember, think of the Practice as a recipe. Now is the time to mix together all the ingredients you've gathered so far and blend them, sample the mixture and become accustomed to what it looks and feels like. Then, just like cooking, you will soon know to add a pinch of this and dash of that to maintain just the right consistency all day.

Of course, there is a word to describe a dedicated practice period of effective creating thinking—and thank goodness, because this is quite a mouthful. It is called visualization.

WHAT IS VISUALIZATION?

Visualization is a popular and widely used term. It doesn't refer to any process in particular. It's more of a catchall word used to describe any one of a number of different techniques and methods for using our thoughts effectively—and Step Four is certainly designed to do just that.

Visualization also tends to imply a dedicated period of practice. If someone says, "I'm visualizing," we generally understand this to mean that the person has purposefully set aside time in their day to practice a more effective process of creative thinking—which again, is exactly what we intend to do here in Step Four.

Visualization, then, is a fancy word to help us distinguish *effectively* creative thoughts from our *regular*, often hit-and-miss, creative thoughts. And within the context of this Practice, it helps us distinguish between our regular day-to-day Practice and the deliberate period of focused exploration here in Step Four.

For our purposes, visualization is clearly defined as being the combination of Steps One, Two and Three.

To visualize, you simply sit down for fifteen minutes or so, close your eyes and do nothing else but concentrate the power of your mind by combining Steps One, Two and Three. You simultaneously control, organize and elevate your thoughts and energy. And as you do, you memorize the experience with an eye toward thinking in this manner all the time, minute to minute.

Visualization is Both Practice and Preparation

As you can see, Step Four is not so much a new step in itself, as it is a combination of the previous three steps. It's intended as both practice and preparation.

When you visualize, you spend quiet, uninterrupted time concentrating the power of your mind and experiencing your inherent creative force so that you can call forth the same thoughts and feelings throughout the day. This is preparation for a more meaningful purpose: to continuously experience yourself as co-creator—an artist actively moulding and shaping the conditions around you into beautiful and unique expressions.

Perfect Practice Makes Perfect

Of course, practice doesn't make perfect, only perfect practice makes perfect. Therefore, we want to be sure that we're applying the steps effectively. Visualization will assist us in doing just that. As we visualize without interruption or the many distractions that bombard us throughout the day, we can concentrate and assess the quality of our thoughts. For example, we can quickly monitor whether or not we are enjoying the experience or struggling to control our thoughts.

Therefore, visualization not only provides us with a platform upon which to practise, but it also acts as a gauge against which to judge our success.

And of course, any time we think more creatively, we're speeding up the process of manifestation. This means that the speed with which we achieve our desires provides yet another way to monitor the effectiveness of our thoughts.

We might think of visualization like cooking. We cook to create a meal, but if we want the meal to be edible, we need to cook well. Similarly, we visualize to create our desire, but in order for our desire to manifest, we need to visualize well. And of course, just like cooking, the more we visualize, the better we get at it. In other words, visualization is both an end and a means.

Doesn't Visualization Mean Visual Images?

Keep in mind that the term visualization can be somewhat misleading, since the word "visualize" is generally taken to mean, "to form mental pictures." While this is certainly part of the process, it doesn't describe the full process.

Forming mental pictures relates to Step Two of the Practice. In Step Two you spent some time forming mental images. You created a collage and detailed your desire. Therefore, as you engage in visualization, you will exercise Step Two, which means that you will most certainly entertain images of your desire just as you did before, although now, without pen and paper or scissors and tape. But Step Two is only a part of the process. The full process additionally combines all the knowledge and means of Steps One and Three.

I also want to point out that mental images are not limited to things we see. Images include general impressions and ways of describing how something is like something else. They include sounds, tastes, feelings and all manner of details. In other words, visualizing is really just thinking. It's what we do in every minute of the day. We continuously fill our mind with concepts and ideas; we think about a grocery list, replay a song in our mind or recall a friend's phone number.

Simply, we don't need to consider ourselves a "visual learner" in order to visualize.

Theresa considered herself more of a "doer" and was somewhat put off by the word visualize. However, one afternoon, Theresa and I were out for a drive when suddenly she brought the car to a screeching halt, pointed to a window display and announced, "I love that outfit!" I asked, "How do you know?" My friend looked back quizzically, so I explained, "Your mind just sorted through a host of past experiences and details, did a quick compare and contrast and spit out a preference. You visualized, but quickly." I then asked my friend what she thought about the outfit. She said, "The color's all wrong and I would need to find a different pair of shoes." I asked, "What kind? Flats or pumps?" She said, "Red, flats. Oh, and I get your point. I'm visualizing again."

We visualize or think continuously. Even now, you're reading the words on this page, but in your mind, you're forming ideas about my voice as it comes across on paper. You're formulating questions, ideas and feelings. You're visualizing, and for an extended period of time.

The truth is, it isn't that it's difficult for most of us to form mental pictures, review details and consider feelings, it's that it's too darn easy. We visualize so automatically, so readily, so continuously throughout the day that we hardly notice we're doing it.

In short, the term "visualize" denotes only a part of the process, the part we engage in quite naturally throughout the day and the part you've repeatedly applied through Step Two.

With this said, let me share with you a story to illustrate *visualization*, its purpose and importance.

An Illustration of Visualization

Two women, Veronica and Kyle, shared the same desire. They both wanted to manifest their perfect mate, their soulmate.

Each day, both women made time to visualize. They each found a quiet place to concentrate, relax and apply all the steps. They reviewed their understanding of creation and formed mental imagery to visualize the impact of their thoughts and energy on the world around them. They set aside mental clutter. They reviewed the qualities of their higher self and as they felt their energy rise, they began to entertain thoughts about their desire—which Kyle did very well.

Kyle was quite a bit better than Veronica at creating mental images of her desire. She once described for me her mental scenario. "I'm in a room with my dream date at a quiet inn near the seaside. There's a window with a white painted frame. It's scratched and chipped. The window's half open and the eyelet lace curtains are blowing slowly in the wind. I can feel the wind on my ankles as if someone's whispering at my feet...."

Veronica, on the other hand, reviewed her desire more as a list. She would think: I desire a romantic. I want flowers and love notes. I desire to go to the movies. She would then build details around each element of her desire. For example, she would think about the color of the flowers she wanted and what she wanted the love notes to say.

Soon, after about two weeks in total, Veronica met her soulmate! She felt urged to try a new restaurant and, on her lunch hour, met her dream date. Kyle, however, had still not manifested her desire.

Why did Veronica manifest her desire and not Kyle, when Kyle's visual experiences were so much more detailed than Veronica's?

Let me answer this in summary and then take you through Kyle's experience in more detail.

Veronica has lovingly been dubbed the human broom. She immediately makes the effort to sweep aside any negativity, distractions and hindrances as quickly as they arise. She continually works to stay connected to her source and has devised ingenious ways to remind herself of her inner qualities. She bought liquid embroidery and wrote the words of her higher self on her pillow, and she wears a necklace inscribed with each word of her Trueprint.

Veronica has engaged in the Practice for four months and visualizes every day, if only for five minutes. She has trained herself to think creatively all the time. She made a commitment early on to do so for thirty days, and she has done so ever since.

Kyle, on the other hand, admitted that she had experienced immediate rewards and a change in her outlook in the first week of her Practice and thereafter simply hadn't put much effort toward Steps One and Three. As a result, she was still allowing herself to become embroiled in unnecessary turmoil and gossip throughout the day, and she visualized more to daydream.

In short, Veronica effectively exercised Steps One, Two and Three during visualization, and more importantly, *minute to minute, day to day*. Kyle had primarily focused on "dreaming," while somewhat skipping the "professional" part. Specifically, she was organizing her thoughts, but without elevating or controlling them.

We can dream about our desires until the cows come home, but this alone will not bring our thoughts to a physical level of materialization. You'll recall from Step Two that a clear visual image allows us to organize energy, but we need also to simultaneously elevate and control energy, and we need to do so both as we visualize and at the times in between, throughout our daily life, minute to minute.

Now, let me take you through Kyle's experience in more detail. This will remind you of what you need to do to think effectively—as well as what you need to avoid.

THE PITFALLS OF VISUALIZATION: WHEN IT DOESN'T SEEM TO WORK

Kyle noticed through visualization that she was struggling to control her thoughts. It turned out that she was bothered about a few things at work, but hadn't taken the time to identify the mental clutter associated with these issues.

This is an important point. We may know very clearly what issues, problems and distractions are bothering us, but this doesn't mean that we have clearly identified the dominant, deep-rooted fear that's keeping these issues circulating in our mind. And of course, when such thoughts continue, they disrupt our ability to create.

As we've been discovering, mental clutter is comprised of thoughts that have occupied our mind for some time. They are the seeds of guilt and fear hiding beneath the surface of our problems, issues and distractions. These are thoughts that we believe deeply and that, over time, have developed into powerful mental habits that easily hide from our conscious awareness.

If we visualize while such thoughts go unnoticed, we may think we are projecting our desire but in fact, in a largely unconscious way, it is the energy of our negative thoughts that we are projecting instead. As a result, our desires may take some time to manifest, or we may find that we are attracting more of what we don't want, simply because we are visualizing against a background of negativity.

This was true for Kyle. As she visualized her soulmate, a number of negative associations were collecting in her mind, including a stressful environment in which she had to face difficult people, unpleasant tasks and missed opportunities. Crowding the heels of her desire for a soulmate was a swarm of negative thoughts that went largely unnoticed and ultimately determined the energy she was releasing.

Of course, the opposite may be true. We may control our thoughts quite successfully as we visualize. We may be aware of our dominant mental clutter and, away from the demands and distractions of the day, successfully replace our disruptive thoughts with productive ones and effectively create.

However, following our visualization experience, as we go about our day, we may find that old fears, doubts or even new angers are arising. We may start thinking, "I'm just being silly" or "this will never happen." We may keep changing our mind, jumping from one desire to the next or becoming involved in new upsets and worry. Which means that, here again, minute-to-minute, negative/distracting habits of thought are systematically tearing down everything we've worked to construct.

It is important to remember that creation is taking place all the time, every time we think. Creation is not limited to the times we set aside to engage in a more conscious practice of creative thinking.

Consistently control your thoughts through day-to-day practice of

Step One. This way, in the moment that your thoughts are tugged sideways, it will be immediate and natural for you to steer your mind back to the positive images of your desire and thus keep the majority of your thoughts effective.

Now, let me turn your attention to Step Two. Kyle thought about her desire on occasion but primarily to daydream. It's important to consistently focus on your desire and treat it as a tool for controlling your thinking.

When you select a desire, as you do in Step Two, you choose one dominant image to hold in your mind and concentrate on. You train yourself to control your thoughts towards a chosen focus. And this is not just any focus. It is something that you are highly motivated to achieve and that automatically stimulates your will, faith, expectation and love. It is an image that assembles your emotions, energy, imagination and concentration towards a productive focus with ease.

> Creation is taking place all the time. We must think effectively, abundantly and habitually.

Much more than a tool for daydreaming, Step Two is designed to continuously expand your thoughts and energy, open your mind and train you to think positively, purposefully and productively.

Systematic practice is key. If you consistently focus on your desire, your thoughts and energy will have a laser beam focus that becomes progressively more and more intense.

Finally, Kyle had yet to consistently apply the words, ideas, images and feelings of her Trueprint throughout the day, so it wasn't automatic for her to incorporate it into her visualization experience. It's so important that we consistently cultivate our connection to a higher flow of energy. We want to be sure to be communicating with energy that can quickly respond and transform and manifest our desires. Your Trueprint makes it easy for you to translate a higher flow of energy into action. And if you consistently think, speak and act in line with your higher energy, you keep an open door to your divine center and continuously bring the infinite intelligence into all your creations.

The point to remember here is that, while visualization allows you to spend concentrated time creating your desire, this should really be considered icing on the cake. You want to use this period of quiet, concentrated practice to assess your thoughts and work on applying all the steps in concert, so that it becomes automatic to simultaneously control, organize and elevate your thoughts and energy at all times— *minute to minute, day to day.*

Through Step Four, you will find it easy to apply all the knowledge and means you've gained so far. You will solidify your understanding, and at the same time, expand and go beyond your current accomplishments.

You will soon find yourself, in every minute, effectively orchestrating all the principles of energy to mould and change the conditions of your life. You will find yourself focused on the things you want, eliminating the thoughts you don't want; consequently, you'll create the things you want and eliminate the things you don't want. Eventually, you will become aware of the Divine Source within all things, and you will naturally, unconsciously and continuously experience your true greatness.

You are a conductor before an orchestra of energy.

LEARNING TO SEE AND FEEL ENERGY

Visualization is simple, but preparation makes it special. The knowledge and understanding of energy that you bring with you into Step Four makes a world of difference in how you think. First and foremost, it will automatically lead you to think more effectively. Let me explain.

If you were preparing a recipe in the kitchen, it's unlikely you'd forget an ingredient. The same would be true if you were driving a car—you wouldn't forget to turn the wheel or step on the brake, because the tools or materials would be right in front of you. If you did forget a step, you'd know right away.

But here, you're working with materials that you don't usually see or directly touch. It's easier to forget an ingredient and add in others unnoticed. Therefore, the more you know about energy, the easier it is to see your thoughts as things, real and concrete tools or ingredients that you can work with easily.

Perhaps at first, you'll only imagine energy, seeing it as a latticework of light connecting all things or fine strands of string that you can tug and pull to attract to you the things you want. You might relate to energy as clay that you can mould and shape. You might feel energy, giving it texture or emotion. Or perhaps, like many people, you'll hear energy. Some say it sounds to them like tinkling crystal.

But however you *know* it, the more you work on understanding energy, the sooner you come to see or feel the creative force around you and, thus, the easier it is to create.

The truth is, we would all think so much more creatively naturally if we could physically see the energy within and around us. Imagine being able to see how intimately connected we are to one another and to all things. Imagine seeing how our energy reaches into all things and how our every thought shapes and moulds our surroundings.

The knowledge you give yourself here, through your Practice, will allow you to "see" the substance of your thoughts and of all things, and this will assist you to work with energy just as though you were working with your hands, but with far greater reach and results.

Towards this goal of being better able to see and feel energy, let me share with you several descriptions of the subtle material you're working with, not only as you visualize, but any time you think in a clear and positive manner. I want to introduce you to the *Principle of Creation*, which describes the highly vibratory, subtle energy that makes up our world.

| Thoughts are things.

Each of the following descriptions will start you on your way to forming imagery that you can associate with the control, organization and elevation of your thoughts. These descriptions give the higher-level energy of creation visual and tactile imagery so that you can relate to this level of energy in a more familiar way, through your physical senses. Then, as you spend time thinking on the energy of creation and working with it, you'll come to know it.

Soon, in your own way, you'll begin to feel creation as you think.

THE PRINCIPLE OF CREATION

Indra's Net

During visualization you immerse yourself in the energetic environment of creation, a powerful web connecting you to *all that is.*

Buddhism offers us a beautiful analogy to describe our connection to all things: Indra's Net. Indra's Net is a web of pearls with each pearl containing the reflection of every other pearl.

Think of all the buildings, people, trees and things in our world as millions of pearls, each one a reflection of all the others. Picture the pearls linked by threads of energy that radiate with a divine intelligence. Imagine yourself a part of this web.

Virtual Energy

The creative energy of the universe is energy so fine and formless that it seems to us as being in a virtual state, meaning almost, but not quite. It's energy in effect, but it's not yet expressed as any one particular form of energy. In other words, it is essentially every thing and no one thing at the same time. It's a universal ingredient that contains all the elements of creation.

If such a substance were accessible on the physical level, you could go into a store, buy just this one ingredient and use it to heal yourself, build a home and create a car.

Realize that as you visualize, you are bathed in this energy, energy that has the potential for all form, energy transforming as you think.

A Continuous Sequence of Flickering States

One way of understanding how this pure energy can be everything at once is to think that it's constantly changing at an incomprehensible speed. It's as if, in a space of time quicker than an instant, pure energy changes from one form into another, and then another, and another. It changes into millions upon millions of different forms. In any given moment, pure energy exists as a combination of all qualities and all forms of energy, seemingly all at once.

In fact, particles of energy that we are familiar with behave similarly, changing into different states of existence and then back again. In a blink, a proton becomes a neutron and pion and a neutron changes into a proton, and on and on.

Energy is constantly changing. And the energy of creation changes, such that it exists as a combination of all things, all at once. Imagine! To put this into perspective, this would be like you, in the blink of an eye, changing into another person and then another and another, until you had changed into every person on the planet. Then, in the next instant, you would change into all people again, and then again and again. In every moment you would exist as a combination of all people and be everywhere and know everything, seemingly all at once.

Energy as Pure Essence

Another way of picturing the all-encompassing nature of pure energy is to think of it as a fluid-like substance, where any one part contains all parts.

Think of a glass of water. It's made up of hundreds of individual drops of water, but together, these drops form a single unified essence.

You could spill out just one drop, and it would be a tiny complete representation of the greater mixture.

In much the same way, the particles of pure energy are so intimately linked with one another that one particle isn't distinguishable from the rest and any particle contains the qualities of the whole.

This interconnectedness explains how energy communicates or shares information so quickly and without signals. Changes to one particle of energy are simply reflected in the whole. Again, you can picture this if you think about putting a drop of food coloring into a glass of water. Very quickly, all the water is colored by the dye.

Energy as a Hologram

Finally, pure energy is perhaps best described using the analogy of a hologram. You can usually find a hologram in the corner of a credit card or driver's license. It's the tiny piece of foil that shows a picture, perhaps your photo or a scene from nature. What's interesting about a hologram is that, if you cut it up into the smallest of pieces and then shine a laser beam on even the tiniest piece, you will still see the entire original picture.

Similarly, just one tiny bit of pure energy contains all the wisdom and power of the universe.

Pure energy is a universal storehouse of abundance.

The Abundance of Energy

To get an idea of just how abundant pure energy is, think of this: it has been reported that if we could grasp just one cubic centimetre of pure energy, we would be holding energy equal to that in a million, million tons of uranium.

The sea of energy in which you live and have your being is literally teaming with potential and power.

Pinch together your index finger and thumb and look at the small space between your thumbnail and fingernail and think about the abundance of power and wisdom that rests untapped in this tiny area of space.

Abundance is an understatement. There is more than enough energy and power in a single breath of air to make millions of dollars, stay healthy and youthful, happy and fulfilled for many lifetimes.

The Metaphorical Clay of Creation

It is out of this vast, abundant matrix that energy is condensed, or essentially squeezed out, and particles emerge. These particles absorb energy and evolve or grow and eventually collect together to form all manner of things.

In other words, everything that exists, every atom and molecule, every fibre of your being, is an extension of creation.

TAPPING INTO CREATION

The highly vibratory, subtle energy of your thoughts is an extension of the highly vibratory, subtle energy of your true being, which is an extension of the highly vibratory, subtle energy of creation—the energy in *all that is*. So it is that the energy all around you is responsive to the energy of your thoughts, because they are one and the same.

And as you have the unique ability to control your thoughts—you can choose what to think and where to direct your energy, raising, or indeed lowering your consciousness—you can control your interaction with the energy around you. You can mould and shape the subtle substance that is your physical reality.

Your thoughts connect or, more aptly, reunite you with everything. You are not separate from anything. You are not apart from the things you wish to manifest. All that you desire is already a part of you, existing within you, in the abundant, interconnected, subtle energy of creation. You simply need to extend your thoughts,

> Everything you could ever want exists in the abundant creative energy within you.

extend creation, which is your gift, and allow the creative force of the universe to bring the substance of your thoughts to a level of material reality.

This is why the focus of our Practice has been to take control of our thoughts, connect with our higher mind and elevate our consciousness. When we do this, we literally think ourselves into resonance with the pure energy within and all around us. We attune ourselves with creation and tap into an infinite storehouse of energy that we can use to create our desires—heal, energize and strengthen our bodies, access songs, inventions and all manner of creative ideas, and receive intuitive guidance and knowledge.

When you visualize, you immerse yourself in the pure energy within and all around you and access the raw building materials that allow you to quickly build your ideas into form.

As you visualize, the currents of thought that flow through your mind spread through the entire ocean of energy to flow back to you as a tidal wave of wisdom, intuition and desires made manifest.

METHOD
COMBINING STEPS 1, 2 & 3

The following Method will guide and prompt you through two visualization sessions. The first is an active form of visualization wherein you actively communicate your intentions to the energy around you. The second session is a passive form of visualization wherein you receive the communication of your higher mind.

I recommend that you read through each session and then do one of several things.

Initially, you may wish to focus on only one key prompt. For example, you may wish to concentrate on the first prompt, which will guide you to relax. You can work on quieting your mind and body and then, in a later session, you can incorporate additional points. Another option is to highlight all the key prompts and additional suggestions that appeal to you and record them, playing them back so you can progress through the session without interruption. Find what works for you.

Keep in mind that each of us will go about visualization somewhat differently. For example, you may be urged to experience the energy around you in a particular way. You may see colors or hear sounds. You may also find it useful to breathe in a particular manner. Don't put pressure on yourself to experience or do something in an exacting way.

The point is to spend time controlling, organizing and elevating your thoughts and energy. Practise to be aware of your thoughts and direct them toward a particular objective. Communicate the particulars of your desire to the energy within and around you. Elevate your energy. You should feel good during and afterward, as though you have been actually living your desire.

Remind yourself that visualization is practice. You needn't accomplish everything at once. For example, you may not "hear" sounds or "see" images at first. That's fine. Know that it's enough to hold these ideas in your mind.

You may find that it's initially challenging to simply sit and relax your mind and body. Other times, you may find it more challenging to conjure up certain sensations. And still other times, you may find that both the details of your desire and further imaginings happen almost simultaneously and with ease, but concentration is easily lost. Give yourself time to develop your gifts. Remind yourself that creative thinking is a skill like any other, but one that is given little emphasis in our daily lives.

Indeed, we go through life concerned about our physical and intellectual development, but comparatively little attention is paid to our emotional and psychic or mental development. Thus, it's reasonable to expect that it will take a few sessions to feel completely confident with combining our thoughts and energy.

However, you will find yourself progressing quickly. Remember, the steps work very well together to condition your mind, body and spirit. Each time you make the effort to carry out even one step in the Practice, you are developing your mind to respond quicker and more effectively with each successive step.

As a final point, remember that we engage in forms of visualization quite naturally throughout the day. The only difference here is that you are making the effort to welcome a greater flow of energy and clear away any distracting stimuli and mental clutter so that you can focus the power of your mind effectively.

Let me invite you now to begin a session of visualization. I have included a number of italicized sections throughout to offer additional suggestions for carrying out key points. And you'll find a review in the reflections section at the end of the chapter so that you can quickly glance at key prompts each time you visualize.

ACTIVE VISUALIZATION

Set aside twenty to thirty minutes to complete the following session. The actual visualization can take as little as a few minutes, but initially you will want to give yourself some time to bring your mind and body to relax.

1. TAKING YOUR SEAT. To begin, you will enter into a quiet period of deep reflection in which you can let go of the physical restraints of your body and concentrate the power of your mind.

Find a quiet place where you won't be disturbed and where you can put your mind and body at rest. Your mind needs to be relaxed, almost like giving up or giving in, so it becomes ready and open to whatever you put in it. If you are desperate or trying too hard, you will defeat the purpose.

Make yourself comfortable. You can sit on the floor, cross-legged, spine comfortably erect and alert. If you like, tuck a cushion just under your tailbone. This will help to ease any tension in your hips.

If you prefer, sit in a chair and sit up straight. Make sure that the back of the chair is comfortably supportive. You may wish to place a cushion behind your lower back. You can rest your hands on your thighs or in your lap, palms facing up.

You may wish to lie down with a pillow, rolled towel or blanket under your knees to relieve tension from your lower back. Rest your arms out to the sides, palms up, just slightly away from your body, making sure your shoulders are relaxed and not hunched forward. It may help to pull your arms up a bit and feel your shoulders roll back and melt down into the floor or bed. You can also rest your hands on your stomach area, palms down, thumbs and index fingers touching, to form a diamond shape around your belly button or lower abdomen.

This preparation is well worth it. Energy flows through your body in a vertical system. Keeping your spine elongated allows for a more natural flow of energy.

2. QUIETING YOUR MIND AND BODY. Turn your attention to your breathing. This will help you settle your mind and focus. Concentrate on filling your belly with air, then your ribcage and shoulders. Then release the air by sinking your stomach inward, compressing the air up and out of your lungs.

It isn't necessary to breathe in any particular manner. But giving your breath attention introduces a focus to start the relaxation process and it will help you concentrate. Remember, you are creating even now. Visualization simply structures and enhances what you do every minute of the day to achieve results quicker and more accurately.

We tend to hold a great deal of tension in our body, because we take shallow breaths much of the time. You can energize your body on a regular basis by breathing in and out with full, deep breaths. Fill your belly, expand your rib cage and raise your shoulders, then exhale deeply by pulling your abdominal muscles in towards your spine.

If you wish to generate comforting warmth, breathe in and out through your nose to help keep heat in your body.

For seven breaths, make a conscious effort to relax your body, starting with your feet, lower legs and the muscles in your thighs and hips. Relax your lower body against your spine. Relax your chest and shoulders, your throat and facial muscles, ears, scalp and, finally, your arms, wrists, hands and fingers.

Many people find it easier to maintain concentration by keeping a controlled, rhythmic breathing throughout their visualization. I personally continue to concentrate on my breathing, but I find that as I become more focused on my desire, my breath naturally falls into a comfortable pattern.

3. CLEARING YOUR THOUGHTS. As you continue to take deep, relaxing breaths, turn your attention to your thoughts. Allow your thoughts to come and go. Allow images and ideas to flow through your mind. As you do, begin to identify each thought. Allow each positive thought to linger for a moment and then let it go and accept the next image or picture that comes into your mind.

Identify each distracting thought. Give it a name as you did in Step One. In your mind, tell this thought that you accept and acknowledge it. Tell this thought that you understand its need to be present, but tell it that you choose now to set it aside and replace it with another.

One of the best exercises I've come across to assist with quieting the mind is the "Tree of Monkeys." If you find it difficult to relax because you can't stop unrelated thoughts from circling in your mind, imagine your thoughts like monkeys in a tree, jumping from branch to branch, swinging wildly. Imagine that each monkey is a different thought and, one by one, acknowledge the thoughts, bringing the monkeys to settle on the branches until all the monkeys are sitting quietly and you can imagine only the rustling of the leaves in the tree.

4. FOCUSING ON THE CONCRETE REALITY OF YOUR THOUGHTS. Now it's time to turn your attention to the energy around you. This will help you to start forming mental images and be aware of the concrete substance you are working with as you visualize.

In your mind's eye, picture the energy all about your body, rushing toward you from all directions, flowing into you as you breathe in. You might imagine the energy as small particles or wind, or see color, mist or light.

Imagine the energy all around your body, about an inch from your skin. Give the energy a tactile sensation or feel. Concentrate on feeling the warmth of the energy. Feel it as a dewy blanket of fog, wrapping you in security. Picture the energy moving around your body, vibrating or swirling around you.

For several more breaths, feel the energy rushing in through the bottom of your spine as you inhale, flowing upward and filling the space in the center of your head at the level of your ears just behind your eyes. Then, as you exhale, project the energy out of your head, allowing it to spread outward in all directions.

Give the energy color. As it enters your body, imagine it takes on a pinkish hue and visualize it pouring from your head to fill the space around you in a haze of blush, bright light, moving and swirling, like smoke filling a glass tube.

With each breath, project the energy farther away from you to expand even beyond the room or space you are in, passing through windows and walls, extending outward into the world.

5. INTRODUCING SOUND. Take several more deep breaths and focus your attention on sound. Listen to your breathing, the air and energy drawn through your nose or mouth and up through your spine. As you exhale, project the energy outward. Give it sound as you imagine it rushing to fill the space around you. Hear it as the sound of tinkling crystal or chimes. Hear it as a faint buzzing sound or music.

For a few breaths, try making an audible "mmmm" sound as you breathe out. Feel the vibrations resonate in the center of your head, between your ears. As you feel these vibrations, concentrate on imagining and feeling the energy around you taking on this sound, picking up movement, vibrating quickly as it spreads outward.

> *You may find it preferable to make an audible "ahhhhh" sound as you breathe out and imagine the same sound as you breathe in (hear it in your mind). This is a very powerful sound. Throughout history, around the world, this sound has appeared in the name given to the creator. Think of the word "God" or "Allah" or "Siddha." It is considered the sound of creation. It's the sound you make naturally when you yawn and release tension from your body.*
>
> *You might also try chanting "om" seven times as you exhale, and then, silently in your mind, seven times as you inhale. This produces an interesting sensation that grows more powerful as you continue to use it.*

6. RAISING YOUR VIBRATION. Begin to review the qualities of your soul from your Trueprint, the bountiful expressions of your higher self. With each quality you think about, imagine the energy deepening in color. Begin to notice that the color all around you, and in you, is bathed in a bright, warming, pink cloud that continues to emanate from your mind, extending infinitely outward. Imagine that you begin to dissolve into the pure energy all around you.

Continue to picture the energy moving farther away, wafting outward, moving far beyond you, to atop buildings. In your mind's eye, watch it slowly settle, caressing all things and all people as it covers and envelops them. Imagine the faces of people change and become pleasant. Notice the light of your energy brightening the streets. See your energy as love. See it washing over the world, purifying, bringing light and warmth to everything.

A very effective exercise to elevate your thoughts is to imagine the energy lifting you so that you gradually rise to meet the top of a mountain.

With each breath, imagine the energy rushing back to you stronger each time, more dense and quick. Feel yourself being lifted as the energy flows beneath you, gently elevating your whole being. As you feel yourself hovering with the energy, indivisible from it, picture yourself floating as high as you like.

You might also imagine the energy as an intense light inside your mind. See it as a brilliant white color, sparkling all around you like sunlight streaming through the trees. Try to fill the entire scope of your inner vision with a bright light, as if you were looking directly into the sun.

Continue to play with the energy you're envisioning, moving it, drawing it inward, projecting and directing it with your mind.

7. IMAGINING YOUR DESIRE. Now, using your imagination, start to picture your desire. Recall your manifestation collage and the details of your desire.

Let your imagination fill in color, sights, and sounds. Feel things, imagine smells and associated tastes. Bring your desire to life with as much detail as possible. Zero in on particulars; analyze and enjoy them.

Picture your desire slowly taking shape.

You may find it easiest to imagine your desire like a movie, projected onto a screen before you, just beginning to play. Or you may see yourself as a builder constructing each element of your desire.

As your image comes to life, draw yourself into the experience and imagine yourself living your desire. Let your imagination flourish.

Concentrate on every detail of your desire for as long as you can. By keeping your imagination active you will be more successful at holding the scene in your mind at length. It's easy to become distracted or simply lose the image or become occupied with some wholly unrelated picture.

If you are concentrating on seeing yourself well and happy, you may find it easier to maintain this image if you create action. See yourself laughing, perhaps running. Then, continually bring your focus back to one image in particular, that of your face, arms, legs or breathing, whatever is the most desired point of change.

If you are picturing your soulmate, greet them, kiss them, move around, but return your thoughts often to distinct and desirable details. The longer you can hold the picture without change, the more rapidly it will form.

To understand the clarity of faith upon which to approach this skill, realize that a similar apparition is beginning to form outside of you as you concentrate. You are conceiving your desire in energized form. Each minute that you hold the scene in your mind, your desire gathers more energy for creating itself.

8. LETTING GO. When the image is gone, intentionally or not, let it go. Do not continue to review bits and pieces of the scene or ruminate on feelings or additional ideas that might start cropping up. For just a few moments afterward, keep your eyes closed and give yourself a break, returning your mind to your breathing.

If you mentally pick and pull at pieces of your image once it's gone, you are withdrawing the energy from your creation and pulling it back to its origin. Allow the energy to go, to detach from you. Every thought is like giving birth. When the miracle of creation happens, cut the umbilical cord. Then, after a few moments, you can return to your creation.

If you like, conclude your visualization session with an audible sound. You may like to try "Namaste" (Nah-Mah-Stay), which is Sanskrit and means that the light in you acknowledges and celebrates the light in others. Or try "Amen," a Hebrew word meaning, "Yes!"

9. ABSORBING YOUR VISUALIZATION. Following your visualization session, take a few moments to review the feelings and sensations you experienced. Absorb these sensations so that you can recall them throughout the day.

I have seen the effects of visualization materialize in a matter of hours. It can also take as long as several months for more complicated desires. As long as the essential ingredients are present—you control, organize and elevate your energy and have complete and abiding confidence in your ability—results are assured.

> As you become aware of energy and handle the tools of thought with care and joy, you will find your entire life changing for the better.

WATCH FOR CUES

In response to your Practice of visualization and the other steps, you will be led intuitively in your daily life to follow the attraction of your energy to where the energy can best move, change or accomplish your anticipated result.

Remember, there are no coincidences. Pay attention to people in your life, strangers you bump into, people you see while stopped at a red light. Notice things that come into your life, that arrive in the mail or things you see while out walking. Pay attention to words you hear.

For example, Tina finished visualizing and went for a walk. Along the way she met a man who asked her for the time. When she told him, he responded, "Great, I have time to pick up a lottery ticket." Tina had been focusing on manifesting money, so she decided to go and buy a ticket.

There was a store across the street and one at the end of the block. Tina was trying to decide which store to go into when she tripped over a bottle cap. "Imagine," as Tina said, "how do you trip over a bottle cap? It's so small. But I did." She picked it up, looked inside, and written on the rubber sealer were these words: "You are on the right track." She purchased a lottery ticket in the store at the end of the block and won!

These cues can indicate the inception of your desire. They are often signposts of your higher mind. And they are often clues to the true essence of your desire.

You think you desire money, but the true essence of your desire might be that you want a break. You want the freedom and time to relax that you imagine money will bring. And it's the true essence of your desire that will be communicated to the energy around you. As a result, you might win an unexpected trip or find yourself directed to take a holiday. Your boss might suddenly suggest that you take a long weekend because things are slow at work. You might receive a discount to a weekend spa retreat in the mail. Or your friends might suggest taking a trip together.

By paying attention to the people, things and events in your life, you begin to cultivate your intuition. You'll likely discover many unexpected manifestations in your life that are steering you in the direction you truly long for, perhaps in response to a deeper desire.

Remarkable Results Through Visualization

Shauna decided to cut out a picture of a beautiful bouquet of roses, frame it, and place it on her desk at work. She decided, then and there, to welcome love into her life. Toward that end, she visualized each day at lunch.

Not long after she set the picture on her desk, she met her soulmate, and each month of their partnership he sent her a dozen roses tied into the most gorgeous bouquet with ribbon.

This is not so remarkable in itself, but her beau, having never seen the picture in her office, matched the roses in color and quantity. Even more remarkable was that the picture displayed a uniquely inscribed ribbon, with the word "love" repeatedly woven into the fabric. On the ribbon of her real roses, her lover had written the word "love" with a calligraphy pen so that it almost perfectly mirrored the ribbon in the photo. This woman's paper roses became real ones.

Steve wanted to earn more money. As he explained it, he felt that he did more work than, or at least an equal amount to, several individuals in positions above him. After reviewing the steps in the Practice, Steve decided to focus on obtaining a raise.

Steve prepared a "blueprint" and set a schedule of visualizations. Every day he envisioned asking for the salary and being given it. He stated the amount over and over to himself, out loud, in the morning and at night, explaining to the universe why it was logical to receive the increased salary.

A couple of weeks later, he awoke, and by the time he drove to work, he realized that he was about to go in to his boss's office and request a raise. I say "realized" because, as he described it, he simply knew this was what he was going to do, although he had not planned to do it this particular day. He simply expected, in each of his visualizations, that the salary would come.

As Steve headed toward his boss's office, he found his boss in the hallway in a great mood, speaking in a very animated and upbeat fashion. When he saw Steve, he started to praise him. Remarkably, he seemed to list every reason why Steve deserved a raise, even in the same order as Steve had laid them out in his visualizations. Steve was so pleased that he went back to his office and finished the day feeling rewarded. His intention to request a raise simply left his conscious thought.

The next morning he was called into his boss's office where, with no pomp or circumstance, his boss pushed a piece of paper toward him and stated that he was to receive a salary increase retroactive to January 1st of that year. Steve's annual salary was now almost $18,000 more than it had previously been.

MAINTAIN YOUR COMMITMENT TO CHERISH YOUR THOUGHTS

You will see immediate results from your visualization sessions. You will likely gain an immediate lift in your emotions and numerous smaller beneficial changes in your life. But do not abandon your Practice. Keep your commitment to yourself. Make time to visualize for a few moments each day. We slide so easily into negative energies. Continue to be alert for any signs of negativity and immediately monitor what you allow to occupy your thoughts.

Indeed, the most important thing to remember is that thoughts are things, living matter. Every thought held in your mind immediately begins to reproduce in the events, people and objects you experienc

For example, if you think, "love," suddenly all similar vibrating energy rushes to meet your mental command and will eventually evolve to a physical representation of love.

Think of your thoughts like this: hundreds of chickens are running around in their pen and you walk in and throw down some feed. Suddenly, every chicken stops, turns and races toward you. Similarly, your thoughts feed the energy around you and energy immediately races to meet your commands.

Cultivate Your Soul Perception: Receive and Know the Answers to Life's Questions

In addition to the active form of visualization in session one, where you purposely concentrate your thoughts towards your desired objective, you can engage in a passive form of visualization. You can simply sit back and benefit from your elevated state of consciousness, allowing your higher mind to bring you ideas, innovations and inspiration.

Passive visualization is particularly useful if you don't know what to ask for or visualize. With passive visualization, you become the listener and allow energy to communicate with you, rather than you imparting your intentions. In fact, during this time, you can bring specific questions to the attention of your higher mind and receive guidance. You might ask, "what should I desire?" Or, you can inquire as to your life's purpose at this time, contributions you may make in this lifetime or life lessons you should specifically pay attention to.

You should inquire in the same manner as you would if speaking with your best friend. If you ask, "what should I do?" your friend is likely to respond, "in regards to what?" If you ask, "Where should I go?" your friend will likely say, "do you mean today? On holiday? What are we talking about?" Be specific. Or simply say, "I am here to listen. Is there anything you wish for me to be aware of?" Or, "Do you have a message for me?"

Passive visualization is an opportunity to explore the vast regions of the collective consciousness and familiarize yourself with the sensations you experience mentally, emotionally and physically in this deeply attentive state so that you can carry these sensations into all that you do.

Thus, passive visualization is not without focus or purpose. You may decide to use it to focus on *being* in the moment. You can concentrate on Step One and simply spend time becoming more attentive to what fills your mind. You might also use passive visualization to focus solely on Step Three and become better acquainted with your higher self or mind and inner voice and wisdom.

With passive visualization, you deliberately cultivate your intuition—your soul perception. Intuition is best described as the immediate knowing of something without conscious thought. You may have experienced your intuitive ability when you met someone for the first time and immediately had a sense that you should or should not pursue a friendship with this person. Or, you may have had the feeling at one time that you just shouldn't go somewhere and later your feelings were confirmed.

A young couple I know were on their honeymoon in a city with a very active nightlife. They loved to party and stay out late. They made a point of stopping in at a local hotspot close to their hotel every night before turning in. They never missed a night, except for one night when they simply felt they should stay in. That night, the nightclub was bombed.

Passive Visualization

1. Begin to visualize as you did in the first session. Sit or lay down in silence and leave behind any distracting stimuli, mental clutter, and the constraints of your physical surroundings.

Metaphysics has long taught that the area in the center of the brain is a bridge to our higher mind. When we take the time to simply "be," to sit quietly for a time and still our mind, we increase activity in this higher center and leave behind the physical world. Interestingly, imaging studies that record activity in the brain during meditation indicate an increase of activity in the area of the brain near the pituitary gland, which is located in the center of our head between our ears. At the same time, it appears that areas of the brain responsible for processing much of the sensory information around us essentially shut down.

2. Think about the spiritual qualities of your higher mind as you defined them in your Trueprint. Give yourself a few minutes to allow these qualities to bring you a sense of peace, security and happiness. You can also concentrate on creating within you the sense of love, faith and expectation, the elevating mental emotions of desire. Allow any or all of these dynamic emotions to fill your mind and let them trickle into your body until you feel warm, relaxed and at ease.

It may also assist you to reach your higher mind if you recall a moment when you witnessed a miraculous vision or event, perhaps a rainbow or the sun shining brilliantly on a mountain range when the air felt perfect. Or recall an inspiring piece of music or an event that moved you. Any experience where you were deeply moved will help unite you with your inner spiritual source.

Many people construct a meeting place or sanctuary in their mind's eye, where they can go to be still. (This is a particularly excellent tool for children to use during visualization or prayer.) You might envision your favorite spot, somewhere you love to go, perhaps in a park. Or, you can create an imaginary setting.

Sit still for a while, content to simply be, and imagine that you can feel a calming, warming energy washing over you.

Tell yourself that, for the next few minutes, everything is perfect. Nothing exists but you and the sensations of your breathing and contentment. You don't have to do anything. Nothing has to happen. Simply sit still and enjoy the silence and peace.

I am my perfect, whole and complete self.

3. When you are completely relaxed, ask your higher mind for the answers you seek: "What desire should I focus on?" "How can I get the money I want?" "How can I solve this difficulty in my life?"

If you have a decision to make, you can bring to your higher mind the two courses of action and wait for the answer: "Should I go or stay where I am?" "Should I take this job or the other?"

4. Allow your mind to fill with whatever comes. Let images, sounds, ideas or feelings come and go. You will likely feel that your thoughts are jumping from one place to another, as if you're watching a variety of unrelated video clips pass across your mind. Just go with each thought until it changes and be unconcerned with what fills your mind.

You may feel as though you are struggling to keep your thoughts positive and relaxed. Your thoughts may gravitate toward difficulties in your life. You might start thinking about a particular person. You may become focused on sounds around you or sensations in your body.

If you feel your thoughts being tugged by negative images, events of your day or some distraction around you, acknowledge the thought as if you were thanking someone for coming to visit, and return your mind to ideas of love and the higher qualities of your soul. Concentrate on dynamic images, feelings and emotions associated with these qualities to momentarily restore your mind to harmony with your higher self.

5. Do not prejudge your experiences and expect a specific response, such as an inner voice, image or other sensation. The answers don't always come in a direct sense at first. It may take a few sessions for you to get a sense of how you experience your soul perception. You may even feel as though nothing has come to you, but don't allow yourself to concentrate on this. Instead, simply allow yourself to *be* for a time and enjoy a few moments of stillness.

6. No matter what happens, try to visualize for at least ten or fifteen minutes. On occasion, work your way up to twenty minutes or a half hour to deliberately cultivate your intuition.

7. When you feel that you can no longer sit or remain lying down, get up and return to the activities of your day and the other steps in the Practice.

Receiving the Answers of
Your Inner Voice and Wisdom

The answers to the questions you ask during passive visualization often come later, as you move about and come into contact with people and things. An answer may come in the form of a letter or telephone call. You may overhear someone speaking and hear just the answer you need. You may "accidentally" bump into someone who offers you the answer you desire. You may feel prompted to do something, or feel that you are being nudged in a particular direction. Or, you may hear the answer you need in a song or see it in a scene you witness.

At first, you may not believe the things your higher mind is telling you. It can sometimes feel as though you are receiving too many answers at once, receiving numerous ideas, innovations, visual images or sounds during or immediately following your visualization. Most people find that it takes a few deliberate sessions to connect with their higher mind and get a stronger sense of their inner urgings.

With consistent practice, you will likely find that even your dreams at night are working to bring you answers. Your night dreams may be filled with the images you have been exposed to during your periods of visualization, although now more detailed and understandable.

You will encourage intuition and the connection to your higher mind by living every day in line with your desires and soul qualities, and by maintaining pure thought. As you successfully integrate each of the steps into your days, you will nurture your higher mind and gain control over your thoughts and emotions. You will eventually fall quite naturally into the most sublime experiences of your soul.

Certainly, every time you visualize, you allow inspiration and intuition time and means to flourish. Intuition is like a personal fireworks display inside your mind, with emerging ideas and innovations exploding into your consciousness.

An example of this in my own life, for which I am truly grateful, is the inception of this book.

A Personal Illustration

One Saturday night, I was sitting at home thinking about all the information that's now in this book. A group of people were coming over the following day to talk about the information and I wanted to give them something they could take home and use as a reference.

I decided to visualize, and created in my mind an image of the participants. I knew what each person desired: a car for one, a better job for another, a partner, a child, and the opportunity to travel. I could see the information I wanted to present, piled neatly in front of each guest. I started to imagine the information stapled, in binders, then spiral bound and in brochures.

Then I let my imagination take over. The information was tied with ribbon and neatly enclosed in boxes labelled "Your best life."

Then the phone rang. It was my neighbor, Kaalyn. He blurted, "I want to know what I want. I want to know that I can get what I want. Would you show me what you showed my mom? She's leaving to live in Florida like she always wanted. I want to learn how to make things happen for me too."

I had met Kaalyn and his mother one day while I was out for a walk and she was raking leaves. We started talking and the next thing I knew I was giving a passionate sermon in her kitchen over Oreos and coffee. She told me that she wanted to live in Florida and I outlined the

Practice to help her obtain her desire. That was two months ago. I had to ask, "What made her decide to go?"

"She met a guy. Like that goofy G.Q. guy in the picture she taped to the wall. Now she's moving to Florida with this guy, not the actual guy, but he's from Florida and he kind of looks like the guy in the picture."

After a moment of silence Kaalyn said, "So, a few friends and I were wondering if maybe you could put all your papers together in a book for us." Kaalyn paused, and I was suddenly lost in a mental picture of a faceless book. "Yes. Okay. I would love to do that. I would really love to do that, Kaalyn."

"Can I drop by tomorrow?"

I was so excited that my next words ran together, "I think I'll need a little more time." I hung up the phone and changed my visualization. I pictured everyone reading a book.

You don't have to worry about the "how" or "when" or "where" of your desire. Visualize your intention and the answers you need will be given to you.

OVERCOMING NEGATIVE HABITS OF WILL

Let me now return your attention to the four elements of desire: will, faith, expectation and love. As you know, these are powerful forces of creation that can work with you to build your desires, or against you, tearing them down. If your will is flip-flopping between fear and doubt and positive beliefs, expectations and love, then you continually expend energy on an internal struggle that simply doesn't need to occur.

As with all the steps in the Practice, visualization can help you gracefully change your *will* so you can enjoy the positive life changes you want. Let me introduce you here to the formula that makes our *will* and show you how you can use visualization to ever-so-gently overcome negative habits of will, release your jailers, develop a strong affirmative will and experience trust, peace and security. And through our discussion, you will see in more detail the relationship among the four powerful elements of creation: will, faith, expectation and love.

Our *will*, remember, is our freedom to choose. It's formed of our expectations and beliefs. For example, if we expect it to rain and we believe it will, then we *choose* accordingly and run for cover or grab an umbrella.

To give you a more dramatic example, I have a friend who expects and believes that there are people trying to hurt him. So he chooses to live nomadically. He lives in a cardboard box and frequently moves around.

What we expect and believe determines our *will*, which in turn determines our *being:* who we are, what we have and what we do in our life.

On the other hand, if we don't know what to expect and we have absolutely no idea what to believe, then we don't know what to do or what to *choose* or *will* for ourselves.

There are several key expectations and beliefs that make up our *will:*

Love or Hate
Success or Failure
Rich or Poor
Live or Die
Health or Sickness
Good or Evil
Happy or Sad
Generous or Miserly
Peace or War

If we expect and believe that both choices are equally valid, then we struggle. Our thoughts go from one set of expectations and beliefs to the next, and we're unsure what to do. We remain inactive, unable to decide, often hesitating to the point that we miss opportunities.

For example, we might say that we *will* to be rich, but we believe that it's equally possible to be poor, and so we hesitate. We might think, "Should I start the business? Should I take this chance?" When one possibility carries as much weight as its opposite, it's difficult to make clear choices, it becomes very difficult to find any motivation and it becomes even more difficult to persist. Why keep going and put so much effort toward something that is only a possibility—on the off chance that it might happen?

On the other hand, when we expect and believe in only one choice, such as success, and accept only one reality and no other, then all of our thoughts and emotions are organized toward a single objective and we act decisively, deliberately, clearly and without hesitation.

For example, if you expect and believe in love and find yourself in a loveless marriage, you don't suddenly change your expectations and beliefs and say, "Well, my partner isn't loving, so now I will expect hate and war and believe in sadness. I *will* this for myself."

Not at all. Instead, if you expect and believe in love, you do all you can to create it. You pursue every avenue, even if it means eventually moving on. And when you imagine finding another partner, you can only imagine a loving partner. It doesn't cross your mind that he or she could be otherwise, because love is the only expectation and belief that has any validity for you.

But here again, if we expect and believe in love and hate, war and peace, happiness and sadness, and see both as equally valid options, then we hesitate and linger, unsure what to do. One option usually becomes a hopeful one and the other dreaded. We hope for love, but we're "willing" to accept hate. And when we picture moving on, the same beliefs and expectations infiltrate our thoughts so that we think, "Well, maybe the next person will be worse."

When we accept both options, we struggle. And conflicting expectations and beliefs in one area of our life tend to affect the other areas as well.

For example, Samuel, a very wealthy man, fell in love and married. Unfortunately, he expected and believed that poverty was always just around the corner and he worried constantly about money. Soon, he became fearful about how "his" money was now further divided by marriage.

His conflict between rich and poor soon led to conflicting expectations and beliefs about love and hate and, further, about happiness and sadness. He started worrying about divorce, and soon his choices and thoughts translated to his actions. He began arguing with his wife as he struggled between these opposing forces.

A man who married with single-minded *will* and chose love, happiness and wealth became conflicted over one set of expectations and beliefs and soon he was struggling in every area of his life.

His wife, on the other hand, continued to nurture her singular, focused, positive *will* for love, happiness and wealth. Though she had no experience, she achieved her most desired job, one that paid well, and she was soon wealthy herself. She refused to nurture anything but happiness and love, and after taking her husband for counseling, she finally moved on and met a wonderful new man.

Looking at the situation from the outside, this woman had every reason to become conflicted herself. Her new marriage was going downhill, she had no job, no experience and her husband's miserly ways were strongly affecting her life. However, she applied the tools, as you are here, to nurture a single, positive set of expectations and beliefs, causing her experiences to reflect only this to the point that she created even greater love, happiness and wealth for herself.

What you expect and believe is what you are willing to accept into your life, and you will create it—you will release a steady stream of energy toward your *will*, and your choices will build your expectations and beliefs into form.

I recall watching an interview with a multimillionaire who was asked how he made his money. He said that one day he was sitting on the floor of his small, empty apartment, poor and brokenhearted, and suddenly he had a realization and started to cry. For the first time in his life, he truly got it: he realized that whatever he truly believed and expected, he could create.

> What you expect and believe is what you are willing to accept into your life.

After that, he never accepted another alternative. He adopted a single, positive will and believed that he was rich, happy, fulfilled, loving and successful and this was all that he was willing to accept into his life, period. This is all that he concentrated on, and shortly after, an idea came into his mind that made him close to a million dollars before the year was out.

If our *will* is divided between two sets of expectations and beliefs, we create images in our mind about being a millionaire, quitting our job, traveling or finding love, but we lack the single-mindedness to build the dream into form. We lack the will, faith, expectation and love that projects a clear and detailed blueprint onto the world to organize the energy around us and orchestrate the conditions of our life.

So, it's obvious to say that a single, positive *will* is important.

However, this is easier said than done, which is why we often use the term "willpower." We can consciously choose health, love and happiness and focus our will toward quitting smoking or being happy, but it doesn't seem to be as easy as flicking on a light switch.

For example, if you smoke and choose to quit, is that it? From that moment on you never smoke again? Or, if you are sad and you choose happiness, are you immediately happy? Why is it often so hard to choose something positive, like "I will lose weight," and harder still to stick with our choices?

It's often difficult to exercise our *will* because it has formed over time. When we make a positive, conscious choice such as "I will quit smoking," the negative expectations and beliefs that we have held over time, like, "I can't. I expect it will be hard. I am a smoker," don't immediately disappear. Instead, old, strong expectations and beliefs tug at our decision and oppose our new intentions.

In short, our will is more of an unconscious habit than conscious moment-to-moment decision making.

DELIBERATE WILL AND HABITUAL WILL

We need to recognize two kinds of will: deliberate will and habitual will. Deliberate will is when we make a conscious choice, such as when we consciously announce, "I am a non-smoker. I will to be smoke free."

Habitual will is when we exercise the same set of expectations and beliefs over and over. Soon, these expectations and beliefs become automatic and we choose things in our life without conscious thought.

We can make a conscious decision any time we like, but our long-standing conditioning may tug us in the other direction. Therefore, we need to know how our long-standing expectations and beliefs formed in the first place.

FORMING OUR EXPECTATIONS AND BELIEFS

Our expectations and beliefs are formed of our imagination and concentration.

For example, if you consistently *imagine* lack, limitation, and fear, you will come to *expect* disappointment and *believe* in failure.

Maybe you've been told the same negative things over and over in your life or been exposed to negative conditions again and again. Eventually, these ideas and images become ingrained in your mind. You become conditioned in favor of negativity and develop a tendency toward it so that it's simply more natural to think, feel and act in a negative manner.

In a way, we become addicted to limiting expectations and destructive beliefs in much the same way that a smoker becomes addicted to nicotine. It's quite automatic and unconscious. A smoker grabs a cup of coffee and it's simply automatic to light a cigarette. In the same way, we wake up in the morning and it's automatic to think, "Oh great. Another day, another dollar." We arrive home at the end of the day and naturally sigh, "I'm tired. I don't feel well." Or we may be called into the manager's office and automatically think, "What have I done?"

What we consistently imagine and concentrate on forms a set of habitual expectations and beliefs. If our expectations and beliefs are negative, they seep into every area of our life until we're sure we'll be late, miss the bus, won't get the raise. Or, as soon as one thing goes well, that can only mean that the roof is about to cave in.

How Can We Change a Negative Habit of Will?

We can change our negative habits in the same way they were formed, using our imagination and concentration to create new and positive beliefs and expectations. This mental pattern of thought, repeated again and again, will translate to the physical, and soon, both the mental and physical act will become automatic.

We can do this in two ways. We can exercise our new pattern of thought in the midst of challenging conditions by using a great deal of strength and effort. For example, every time we want a cigarette, we consciously choose not to smoke. Or, every time we feel negative, we consciously choose to think positive. This option pretty much leaves us back where we started, struggling between *deliberate will* and *habitual will.*

On the other hand, we can use the power of visualization to *imagine* a new set of expectations and beliefs and *concentrate* on them. Repeating this mental act over and over again, we are deliberately cultivating a new habit. The more we perform the mental act, the quicker it will translate to the physical and become a habit of thought, emotion and action.

To give you an example, a young woman was tired of being pushed around at work and was angry with herself for never speaking up. So she created a mental image of herself in meetings saying things like, "That's a good point, I wonder if I could add to that." And, "I disagree, consider for a moment…." She visualized images of confidence and calm, relaxed self-assurance to build new beliefs and expectations. She repeated these mental images over and over again, making them the focus of her thoughts.

About a week later, she was in a meeting with all the department heads, the president and vice president, when she suddenly said, "I disagree. I wonder if I could add...." She left the meeting a little surprised. She had said these words without any conscious mental preamble. They simply came out of her mouth as she had mentally rehearsed them.

As another example, Jason felt negative most of the time. He believed and expected that the world was basically "a rotten place."

Jason started to visualize a different view of the world. He consistently imagined and concentrated on the things that were good in his life and in the world around him.

A few weeks later, Jason was at a party and someone started talking about all the despair in the world and how people were fundamentally rotten, and Jason responded, "Oh come on, the world's not so bad, there's a few bad apples, sure, but what about...." Later, driving home, it hit Jason. He felt different. His view of the world had actually changed and translated into action. He felt "better," more resilient and capable.

The truth is, most people fail to achieve their goals, create their dreams and change negative habits because they simply don't know how to focus the power of their imagination and concentration.

The basic formula is this:

Your Imagination and Concentration =
Your Expectations and Beliefs =
Your Will.

And what thy Will will be done!

Add repetition to this, and you have a habit.

Visualization is simply a graceful form of repetition. It gives us the means to *imagine* new and greater things for ourselves and to *concentrate* on these things so that they become a habitual way of being.

It has been written, "Imagination is the eye of the soul." When you imagine, you see through the eyes of your higher self. You expand the concepts you have about yourself and your life and imagine new and greater ideas about who you are and what you are willing to accept into your life. You break out of the prisons you create with negative thinking and the hell that results in life. You change your conditioning.

> Visualization is simply a graceful form of repetition.

Imagination is a powerful tool. If you can't imagine yourself rich, happy, healthy, youthful, energized, non-smoking, thin or beautiful, how can you become so?

Couple imagination with concentration and you have all the tools to build your dream into form. Concentration means to draw everything to a central point. When you concentrate, you focus all your thoughts and emotions and direct them to the single image you want in life.

When you strengthen your *will*, you don't hesitate or miss opportunities. You are willing to accept more and greater things into your life.

All of which becomes automatic.

It takes very little effort with the right tools to overcome your conditioning and reprogram your *will*. You can change your expectations and beliefs, and therefore your actions, until eventually it's absolutely automatic to be rich, healthy and successful. Every thought, every emotion and every action comes to echo your positive beliefs and expectations and you cannot intend or *will* for less. And what you choose, you create. Your will determines your *being*, which in turn determines what you *have* and *do* in your life.

Visualization is a powerful tool. Combined with the other steps in the Practice, it gives you the means to choose the best for yourself, and to ingrain your choices into your mental thought patterns so deeply that you can only be, act and accept that which you truly desire.

When you visualize, you focus the power of your mind to rewrite your life. And you are working with the most powerful force for transformation—the energy of creation. One tiny effort on your part reaps enormous reward. Plant a single seed and a tree will grow, scatter seeds and reproduce. In time, you simply have more and more of the things you want, and become more and more the person you want to be, quite automatically.

GROUP VISUALIZATION

A group of five people, having learned about the Practice, decided to apply the steps together. Two desired to quit smoking and three wanted to lose weight.

They created ingenious ways of detailing their desires. One woman took a photo of herself and outlined her picture with a black felt marker until she looked as slim as she desired. A computer-savvy man morphed his photo to display his ideal physique. Another woman asked a friend to spend the day with her and take photos showing her drinking coffee, visiting people and eating, all without smoking. She specifically found things to do with her hands to illustrate what she looked like as a non-smoker. One photo showed her outside at a café, waving her hand and crinkling her face to show disdain for a smoker seated nearby.

The group exercised incredible imagination and concentration, finding numerous ways to display a collage of their desires. They committed to visualizing morning, noon and night, if only for five minutes. Three weeks later, both smokers had cut down "unintentionally." As one man said, "I went out onto the balcony to have a tea and smoke, like I always do, and it wasn't until I came back into the house that I realized I didn't have a cigarette." Likewise, the other "non-smoker" reported that she simply didn't "light up" at times when she normally would.

Of those desiring to lose weight, two had lost several pounds and the third person had lost a couple of pounds. One had started walking, something she had never been able to motivate herself to do, but which she had illustrated in her picture wall of desire.

After five weeks, one gentleman had quit smoking. He said, "I was down to less than half a pack from one and a half packs a day, so I decided to get serious," he added with a laugh, "and actually try."

The other smoker was down to five or six cigarettes a day and said, "actually, that's not true because today I've only had two, so there!"

All three who wanted to lose weight had dropped over ten pounds each. And even better, all had incorporated into their lives new habits that they desired. All were eating healthier, exercising as they had planned and doing the things displayed in their photos.

Additionally, all three had achieved at least one other desire. One woman met a partner, who was taking her on a cruise. Another woman won a trip. And one man was reunited with his daughter: "She just called. I never thought she would, but she did, and we shared a meal. Fifteen years of being apart…that's something."

REFLECTIONS ON STEP FOUR
VISUALIZATION

As soon as you rise, repeat your desire. This way, you activate your imagination and concentration, exercise your expectations and beliefs and demonstrate your *will.* Repeating your desire first thing in the morning, you begin with a sort of mini-visualization and accept, anticipate, intend and concentrate on the life you want.

- Make time each day to visualize using the following prompts:

    a. When comfortably seated or lying down, take seven deep, slow, rhythmic breaths, focusing on the rise and fall of your belly, chest and shoulders. Breathe through your nose if you wish to generate heat in your body. Continue breathing and allow your breath to fall into a natural, deep rhythm.

    b. Introduce Step One and begin to identify and acknowledge your thoughts. Set aside any distracting thoughts.

    c. Begin to think about the energy around you. Image it as color, sound, movement—anything that assists you to visualize the flow of energy within and around you. Picture the energy moving up through your spine and into the center of your head, hold for just an instant, and then concentrate on projecting the energy outward as you exhale, like a stream from your mind that flows into the space all around you.

    d. Create an audible "mmmm" or "ahhh" sound as you breathe out, using the vibration of your voice to help visualize the movement and vibration of energy and draw you away from any stimuli around you. Feel the vibrations in the center of your head, between your ears.

e. Now raise your consciousness by turning your attention to the qualities of your Trueprint. Think about a loving experience or sensation and imagine projecting your love out into the world.

Think of yourself like a conductor and continue to play with the energy around you. Feel yourself becoming lighter, lifted in mood and feeling. You may wish to imagine yourself rising with the energy that flows strong all around you. You can rise to the top of a mountain or have the energy carry you to a place that holds special significance for you.

f. From the center of your mind's eye, picture your desire emerging. Enjoy your desire in as much detail as possible and concentrate on it for as long as possible.

g. When the image or idea leaves your mind, let it go and concentrate on your breathing, then bask in the feelings of happiness, contentment and thankfulness that follow a pleasurable event.

• It's normal to find it difficult to visualize for even two or three minutes at a time. I found it difficult to sit for five minutes when I started, but that turned out to be long enough to manifest my desires.

You might visualize for a couple of minutes, relax and visualize again. Over time, you will be surprised to discover that you can concentrate for much longer periods.

Keep in mind that the most important part of the process is how pleasurable the period of visualization is for you. You should thoroughly enjoy every moment in the same way you would enjoy the actual physical manifestation of your desires.

The care you employ at the start, and every effort you make, will condition your mind and body to respond quicker and more effectively each successive time you decide to project your thoughts and create.

In time, five minutes in a parked car or fifteen minutes in the office at lunch will achieve the same results. In fact, you will be pleasantly surprised to find that even thoughts you would have previously considered to be rather fleeting now take on a more purposeful release of energy, and your wishful thinking and daydreams begin to manifest.

Keep in mind that the most important part of the process is how pleasurable the period of visualization is for you. You should thoroughly enjoy every moment in the same way you would enjoy the actual physical manifestation of your desires.

• The more you engage in visualization, the more your overall pattern of thought becomes logical and disciplined. Negative thoughts are more easily replaced and you naturally monitor what you allow to occupy your mind, until even your dreams at night add energy to your desires.

• You will receive immediate benefit from opening your higher creative centers of consciousness. When you consistently allow yourself to attune with the energy of creation, your higher mental or psychic centers act as transformers that tap the collective consciousness. You will receive inspiration and intuition and draw upon the knowledge imprinted on the collective consciousness over centuries.

• You needn't concern yourself with trying to figure out how your desire will be realized. The answers come, even if your desire is not definitive at the moment. All that matters is that you complete the

Steps of the Practice with any desire in mind and allow for the development of your higher faculties.

You will immediately find your life steered in a more positive direction. You will find yourself drawn to rewarding situations, people and the answers you desire. You will pick up a book that falls open to a page with the very information you need. You will run into someone who can assist you in just the manner you require. You will see an ad that answers your needs or hear someone in an elevator discussing the very thing you need to hear. Everything you need will come.

• Many of us have forged an ability to think destructively over the years and have seen this thinking manifest in continual pain and heartache. But it takes very little time to unlearn destructive patterns of thought and replace them with a singular, positive purpose.

We can overcome a negative pattern of thought by using the same means we employed to create it: we mentally repeat a single, affirmative *will* until our thoughts translate to our actions and manifest on a physical level.

Consistently visualize and exercise a new pattern of thought. Build an affirmative will that accepts one path and not the opposing conflicted path of passive wishing. Over time, as your concentration and faith increase, you will build a new structure of thought and your actions and words will fall in line.

• Every small step is really a mountainous stride. When you take one small step in advance of your desire, in thought and action, you fortify the inner tools of creation to use in every area of your life.

One small accomplishment deserves a standing ovation. Maybe you choose carrots over chocolate cake at lunch or put one cigarette back in the pack, but in actuality, you are exercising a new habit of thought that will eventually become an unconscious and habitual way of life.

• As you become more accustomed to visualization, you will come to know the sensations and images that work best for you. You will create your own exercises, following your intuition and the guidance of your higher mind. And, in your own unique way, you will come to "know" energy and your inner creative power.

• The consistent use of each step and the careful, systematic conditioning experienced in each period of visualization will program your entire system until you consistently attract an abundant and rewarding way of life.

• You will benefit from every attempt and gain great rewards from even a little effort.

STEP FIVE
demonstration

The affirmation of faith is an army of action,
willing to sacrifice everything
for silent, unseen intangible belief.
Acting on the invisible,
offering evidence for the imaginable,
as witness to our intention,
we wage a demonstrative crusade.

I now choose to act on my desire.
I am ready,
ready to be as I desire,
to live and move accordingly.
I am ready.
I AM
as I desire.

PRINCIPLES
INVOLUTION

Step Five, *Demonstration*, will give you the means to consistently align your actions with creation. It assembles spirit, mind and *body*, addressing the totality of your being. Through small, simple acts of demonstration, your actions cement your thoughts, which in turn encourage the right action, and so on.

By using demonstration to bring your actions in line with creation, you can be sure that each time you take a step in the Practice, you catapult yourself into the realm of infinite power and possibility, until you naturally find yourself in a state of *involution*.

THE PRINCIPLE OF INVOLUTION

Involution is not a word you'll find in every dictionary. In mathematics it describes an operation that returns the original number. In biology it means to restore to an earlier condition. Both definitions hint at the meaning applied here. *Involution* means to be *restored to a state of creative awareness*.

Think of *involution* much like evolution. But rather than slow, progressive, evolutionary shifts that result in a different form, involution is growing into our selves, and it happens through insight and inspiration. Insight is an instance of apprehending the true nature of something, often in ways that go beyond intellectual reasoning, and it leads us to be infused with spirit or inspiration.

Involution then, is the result of moment-to-moment insights tha transport us in leaps and bounds to our original and infinite self, our essence—an essence that is always just right there, as if beside us!

In one word, involution captures a process of growth and state of being that is the essence of the Practice. An essence, which culminates here in Step Five.

Step Five is living in accordance with involution through demonstrating your desires. It's bringing the whole of your life to reflect a state of creative awareness. Step Five aligns your actions with your thoughts and emotions so that now, what you think, say and *do* will be an extension of creation.

It's so important that we take small, manageable steps throughout the day to align our actions with creation, just as we have done with our thoughts and energy. Otherwise, we can easily think one thing, but say and do another. Have you ever thought, "I don't want to do this," and at the same time, the words are coming out, "Okay, sure. I'd love to." When our actions oppose our intentions we limit and block our ability to create.

I watched a woman on television desperate to no longer live as a "pack rat," obsessively collecting clutter. Yet, at the same time, she was holding what she claimed was her favorite keepsake, a decorative pillow, which she saw every day, embroidered to read, "Princess of Clutter."

It is not enough that we think creatively, because we are a package deal. Our thoughts, emotions and actions are intimately linked. What we do and see, hear and say affects our thoughts, deeply, because we believe what we see ourselves do and say. We are conditioned to accept what we see, touch and feel.

And it's impractical to think that we can separate our thoughts from our actions. We can; we can control our thoughts. But in our busy lives, we don't always have time to monitor every thought. Besides, our goal is to develop a habitual way of being so that even without think-ing, so to speak, all aspects of our functioning serve as support systems for our desires.

WHAT IS DEMONSTRATION?

Demonstration is acting out in small, reasonable ways the parts of your desire that can be immediately experienced.

For example, if you desire a mate, you might go window-shopping during your lunch hour for the perfect first date outfit. You don't need to buy it! Simply demonstrate your desire.

Demonstration outwardly expresses your will, faith, expectation and love. If you go window-shopping, then you outwardly express your will for partnership. You demonstrate that you have faith that you will indeed find a partner. You demonstrate that you expect partnership, because you're preparing for it and you're simply waiting for energy to take care of a few minor details like who and when.

Demonstration expresses that your will, faith, expectation and love have expanded and welled up within you to the point that they are bubbling over and looking for an outlet.

YOU WILL BE LED TO ACT

The truth is, whether you purposefully set out to demonstrate or not, the energy you're generating will nudge and prompt you to act. You will be led toward particular people and events—opportunities—where energy can

> Energy will lead you to where it can accomplish the best result.

quickly reproduce. In other words, if you didn't intentionally engage in Step Five, you would soon find yourself naturally urged to demonstrate!

It's important, however, to purposefully provide an outlet for the energy you're generating because otherwise it can easily be spent in undesirable ways.

For example, have you ever had a day when you were so excited about some event coming up that you could hardly think straight and you found it hard to concentrate on anything? You found yourself "bouncing off the walls" all day, but accomplished next to nothing, so to speak? Initially, you can have a similar experience through your Practice, as you're generating an enormous amount of energy and, at first, this can be overwhelming. You essentially feel great, but you don't know where or how to channel your energy. And energy can easily be channelled in the wrong direction. Janine offers this story.

Janine desired a new job, so she started the Practice. She followed the Practice for a week and reported that she felt "absolutely terrific." A week later she called me to say that she was exhausted. Not only that, she had missed a phone message for a job interview. I asked her to describe what she had been doing for the last week.

The past Monday, Janine was invited out for dinner with friends and accepted. Tuesday, she accepted another invitation. Wednesday another, for drinks and dancing, and as it turned out, the rest of her week was spent partying until the wee hours of the morning. Janine was shocked. She hadn't realized she had been out every night. She commented, "I haven't done that since I was in college. I don't even know how I could do that. I had so much energy. I thought I was twenty again."

The following week, Janine channelled her energies in the right direction through demonstration, giving herself time to become accustomed to the increased energy and her own inner voice or urgings. Eight days later, Janine was offered the job she wanted.

Demonstration Places You in the Path of Opportunity

When you demonstrate, you create a breeding ground of opportunity for energy. As you act, you come into contact with events, people and objects where energy can quickly reproduce. Others may decide to give you what you want as your energy imprints on theirs. Opportunities will arise. You provide energy a cast of characters and different settings with which to quickly orchestrate your desire.

Remember, you are building up an enormous amount of energy through the Practice. You can quickly speed the process of manifestation by giving energy a variety of immediate means to reproduce.

For example, Malina desired a new job, but she wasn't sure what career she wanted. So, she decided to demonstrate her desire by doing a little research. She started out to go to a library, but along the way noticed a second-hand bookstore. She stopped in and the first book she saw was a film industry catalogue called *Reel.*

As Malina flipped through the pages of the book, she became energized by the prospect of working in film. She bought the book and headed home. Just outside her apartment, she ran into a neighbor who noticed her book. The neighbor, it turned out, worked in the film industry and put her in contact with a casting agent.

For the next two months, Malina spent all her spare time working as an extra in various films. Her knowledge of the film industry grew until she could detail most professions within the industry.

One weekend, she had a 5 a.m. call to set. As Malina described it, "there was a hub-bub of activity. I was really helpful! The main actor started joking with me and, the next thing I knew, they were asking me to act!"

The director asked her to say a few words. She spoke directly to the very actor she had featured twice in her picture wall of desire. She was paid an excellent rate and introduced to several influential people.

Four and half months after clipping her first picture and beginning to consciously monitor her thoughts, Malina secured an agent and a role in a made-for-television movie. Malina has jokingly changed her name to Manifest.

Faith and Demonstration

We are very much conditioned to believe what we experience. When we experience even a small portion of what we desire in the outside world, our faith in our desire increases. Our desire is no longer just an idea or image in our mind; it starts to become a tangible reality.

Thus, demonstration of your desire will increase your ability to build bigger mental concepts and expand what you are willing to believe as plausible reality for yourself.

This is not suggesting that you charge a million dollars to your credit card or ignore the advice of your physician and pretend to be rich or healthy. Demonstration is about increasing your attitude toward possibilities, acceptance and faith.

We often fail to accept abundance into our life, because, deep down, we don't really believe our dreams are possible. Demonstration helps us to see that our dreams *are* possible. When we demonstrate, we find plausible ways to express our desire and create realism. And as portions of our dream become real, we start to accept that we are entitled to our dreams and nothing but our own limiting beliefs prevents us from accepting a more bountiful life.

For example, Chris needed almost a thousand dollars to have some work done on his teeth. He had no idea how he was going to get the money, nor did he know how he could demonstrate his desire. Nonetheless, he passively visualized and instructed his higher mind to bring him the answer. Chris followed the practice for three days.

One morning, he was going through his wallet to make sure he had the ten dollars he owed to a co-worker. He was suddenly struck with the idea that he could use this as an opportunity to demonstrate his desire. He decided to return the money, plus ten dollars, saying, "Take it, it's about to come back to me tenfold!"

Chris felt that by giving an extra ten dollars he would witness the reality of his desire in his speech and actions. He felt that this act would demonstrate his faith in himself and the creative power of the universe. As well, it was an excellent way to exercise the qualities of his Trueprint.

That night, a friend called and offered to pay Chris two hundred dollars for two hours of work setting up a banquet. He also received a hundred dollar bill in a birthday card from a friend in Europe. And, the next day, Chris received a four-hundred-dollar bonus at work.

> There are no impossible dreams, just our limited perception of what is possible.
> —*Beth Mende Conny*

Using Demonstration as a Tool to Eliminate Negativity

Demonstration serves another useful purpose. It is a quick, easy, practical way to immediately rid ourselves of negativity and doubt.

Our negative voice often comes disguised as indifference and resignation, saying things like, "I don't care. It doesn't matter. It's no big deal. It's probably not right for me anyway." If you suddenly hear a nagging, procrastinating, self-destructive voice that fears change, act out some small portion of your desire. When you demonstrate, you immediately distract yourself long enough to practice a more productive pattern of thought, quickly whisking yourself toward a positive habit.

The negative voice is strong in all of us, especially when we get close to the finish line and begin to accept the realization of our dreams. This voice keeps us from developing a singular, positive habit of will and leaves us passively wishing. It threatens us with the past, holding us back while projecting us into a similar future. Our negative voice constantly suggests that we might not realize our desire and pulls us toward another focus. All we need to do to overcome this voice is immerse ourselves in our desire and stay focused on the thoughts and emotions that attract abundance. Demonstration, like detailing and visualizing our desire, helps us do this.

Remember, you only have to look after each moment. Stop, grab your coat and engage some small part of your dream. Or pick up a pen and paper or a magazine and demonstrate by writing or reading. By actively carrying out your desire, you quickly repattern your thinking, moving closer to who you want to be.

For example, when I first started to write this book, I was overwhelmed. Suddenly, I was filled with self-doubt and my will was flip-flopping between write and don't write. So, I picked up my coat and walked to the bookstore, intent on demonstrating my desire by immersing myself in research, great works and authors.

When I entered the store, I overheard a woman asking for books on manifestation. I immediately went over and struck up a conversation. Twenty minutes later, I was reinspired and full of faith. Then, just as I was about to leave, a book caught my attention. I picked it up, opened the cover and noticed an email address. I bought the book and contacted the author.

The next day, I received a response saying that the author was traveling home from New York, but would be stopping in my area for a few hours and would be happy to meet with me! When I arrived at the arranged meeting, I began to thank the author, but before I could say more, he held up his hand and said, "Let's take care of you, do you have a pen and paper?"

What you think exists! Every thought is released as an impulse of energy that immediately seeks to reproduce itself. When you demonstrate you simply provide the immediate means for energy to reproduce as a person, event, action or object.

DEMONSTRATION WILL ASSIST YOU TO VISUALIZE

When you engage in demonstration, you practice a physical form of visualization. When you demonstrate, you assemble your concentration and imagination; you elevate your mood, release positive energy and greatly contribute to the construction of your desire.

Demonstration is also a way of collecting associated images that can help to bring realism to your visualization experience.

Images are referred to as dissociated or associated. A dissociated image is an image we view from afar. We are somewhat disconnected from it. Instead of "living" the experience, we are viewing it, like someone in a movie theatre. It's as if we are directing a scene and watching it play out.

An associated image, on the other hand, is an image we experience directly. For example, instead of seeing ourselves on a balcony near the seaside, we *are* on the balcony looking through our own eyes out over the sea, smelling the salt air, listening to the gulls, feeling the sand between our toes. In other words, we are "living" the experience.

When we demonstrate, we put ourselves in touch with sights and sounds associated with our desire, so that our desire falls within our scope of experience. And we can bring these direct experiences of taste, touch, smell, action and experience into visualization so that it becomes more real and effective. When we visualize, we can recall and manipulate true visual, auditory and kinesthetic sensations and draw ourselves into the visualization experience with greater ease. And we can concentrate longer, because we can fixate on "real" details.

By taking action in line with your desire, you increase your association to your desire. It becomes more vivid and "real" during visualization. And when you are adding in actual occurrences, real ingredients, your desire seems more plausible and your faith increases.

You will notice a physiological change as your visualization becomes more detailed and believable, the detailed mental image registering with your body much the same as the actual event. You will immediately receive benefit from an uplifted and enthusiastic state of being. The time you spend enjoying a pleasurable event, be it real or imagined, is promoting well-being.

Becoming Clear About Your Desire

Demonstration is another key to help you know what you want and why you want it.

We often think we want something, only to discover that we really want something else. It's easy to think we will do or say something when we are only imagining it. It's easy to say we want something when we aren't presently experiencing it. It can be difficult at first to trust our inner voice and heart and feel confident that we know what we want and why. Demonstration allows you to experience your desire, almost like a preview of what's to come, so that you can feel confident in your desire or discover more clearly what you truly desire and why.

When you demonstrate, you live your desire fully in your mind and translate your thoughts into action as much as possible. And as you experience your desire, you become clear about what you will, believe, expect and love, and why.

For example, Alex said she wanted money to shop. But as she started window shopping she thought, "you know what? I don't want to shop, I just want the time off." Clark wanted money, but as he started engaging in the activities he associated with increased wealth, he realized that what he really wanted was to leave his current job and find other employment.

Immerse yourself in your desire. Ask yourself, "What would I be doing right now if my desire were realized?" Then ask yourself, "What can I do right now to experience a part of my desire?" If you want to travel, visit a travel agent. If you want improved health, do something you

Ask yourself, "what would I be doing right now if my desire were realized?"

249

associate with better health. Perhaps have a friend bring over a humor-filled video and laugh for a couple of hours.

Certainly, as you demonstrate, your visualizations will become more realistic and you will experience parts of your desire in thought. But, as much as possible, physically align your life with your thoughts. Let the universe know you're ready. See if you can demonstrate just five minutes a day and during that time ask yourself, "If my desire was realized, would I be doing exactly this?"

DEMONSTRATION COMMUNICATES YOUR READINESS TO RECEIVE

Demonstration communicates to you, and to the universe, that you are ready to receive, ready for something more. It brings you to exhibit in body, as well as mind and spirit, that you are truly prepared to live differently.

Many people have desires but do not stop to consider whether or not they are truly ready to receive them. For example, what will you do with the money you manifest? Do you know how you will invest it and spend it? Will you live in the house you manifest? If so, have you accounted for upkeep and property taxes?

We talked about the concept of readiness in Step Two when you started to detail your desire. Part of the purpose of detailing your desire was to prepare yourself mentally, emotionally and spiritually to receive, believe, expect and love your desires. And this detail was used to create a Desire

Are you prepared to live differently?

Statement. This statement communicates to you, and to the universe, that you are ready to receive. Now, demonstration will prepare you physically. And since your actions exhibit your beliefs and expectations, demonstration will continually expand, strengthen and intensify your energy.

Energy, remember, doesn't so much work for you, as it works through you. You need to open the doors and expand your thoughts and energy. Demonstration is bringing you to do so through body as well as mind and spirit.

For example, one gentleman, Gary, desired a windfall of money. He wanted to live, "just once" as he put it, "like a king." So he cleared his mind, visualized and after a couple of weeks, when nothing seemed to happen, he became discouraged.

Then Gary took a look around his apartment and laughed. His feet were propped up on a pizza box, he hadn't cleaned all week and his clothes were crumpled on the floor.

That day, Gary reorganized his life and began to *demonstrate* his desire. He started to live like a "king." He cleaned up his apartment, showered, shaved and made out a list of exactly what he would do with his money. He window-shopped, researched and basically began to live as though he already had everything he wanted.

Two months later, Gary and a friend split the winnings of a charity lottery ticket. Gary invested his portion of the money in a home and, shortly after, sold it for a substantial profit.

Are you ready for your desires? Are you prepared? Are you ready to be healthy? Have a partner? Be in love? Take a better job? Change careers? *Are you really prepared to live differently?*

NOW IS THE TIME TO LIVE

Now is the time to live. Now is the perfect time for you to be happy, healthy, wealthy, successful and fulfilled. There is no better time. If you truly understand that you are a creative force and that your every thought is shaping the conditions of your life, then it is only a matter of time before you physically experience all the things you have imagined.

"Dum vivimus, vivamus."
Let us live while we live.

Begin now to live as you desire and prepare yourself to receive the material expression of your dreams. Don't say, "When I have money…" or "I have to wait until…" or "If only…." Begin now to demonstrate and align your life with your dreams.

METHOD
ALIGNING THOUGHT & ACTION

You can demonstrate in so many ways. If you desire wealth, research aspects of wealth and finance. Educate yourself about real estate, art, literature, investments and anything else you want to spend your money on. Window-shop or pick up second-hand magazines that pertain to your desire. Make a list of charities to which you will donate some of your wealth or list friends you will assist financially.

If you desire romantic fulfillment, act as though you are already involved in your dream relationship. Go to places you would like to visit with a partner. Dress up, prepare a great meal, or take yourself out in the same manner as you envision your dream engagement.

If you want to travel, research the countries you are interested in visiting. Learn the culture, study the language and visit an embassy or museum. Find out about travel accommodations, equipment and clothing you might need, and any necessary arrangements at home, such as canceling subscriptions or deliveries.

If your desire is to lose weight, what is it you expect to do differently? Is there a dream outfit you want to wear? Go window-shopping. Visit gyms or social clubs associated with your desire, just as you have pictured in your mind. Turn on your favorite music at home and have a celebration dance or take yourself out. Research meal plans. Make an appointment to see your doctor and tell him or her that you *are* losing weight and you simply want to know the best way to support your new lifestyle. Act in line with your thoughts.

You can even demonstrate by hanging up a banner that reads, "The solution is on the way." Be creative. Demonstration is one more way to increase your imagination and concentration. In any way you can, experience the parts of your desire that can be immediately acted out. Do what feels reasonable to you. In small ways—in every way possible—live and enjoy your desire.

Make a commitment to spend five minutes a day actively engaged in your desires.

Listen to the Whispers In Your Mind and Heart

Act on the emerging suggestions of your inner voice and the answers and cues you receive. Take a risk and demonstrate, even a little. Experience bits and pieces of your desire and explore the possibilities. If your desire is to open your own business, look at vacant spaces for rent. You don't have to rent one, just see what happens as you engage in actions associated with your desire.

If you suddenly feel moved to take a course in something, do so. If you feel you might benefit from exploring other avenues of employment, create a resume, visualize the interview and make appointments. You don't have to quit your present position.

Take on a volunteer job at something close to your desire or get out and interview people working in your desired role; most people love to talk about themselves and what they have accomplished.

With every interaction comes the possibility of new ideas. Opportunities will present themselves; *you have assured this,* by projecting onto the world a well-formed design. Listen to the tiny whispers in your mind and heart.

Carl wanted a relationship and marriage. He decided to demonstrate by looking through the personal ads in the newspaper, which he had never done. However, before he found the personal section, he saw an interesting advertisement for a one-day course he felt urged to take. He met his soulmate at the course.

Elise wanted to open a salon of some kind. She started demonstrating by going around to various spas and beauty salons and interviewing people. She eventually met a salon owner keen to sell. The owner was so impressed with Elise's dream and the incredible enthusiasm and detail of her desire that she offered to work out a financing arrangement to eventually turn the business over to Elise.

Jasper wanted a house. She felt so energized by the Practice that she boldly drove to the neighborhood of her dreams and demonstrated by knocking on doors and inquiring about the area, schools and places for sale.

She met an elderly lady with no family or friends. Jasper was so taken aback by this older woman's loneliness that she returned every Saturday to clean, do yard work, have tea and visit. In a few weeks, she was tending to a couple of homes, at times accepting small gratuities, mostly in the form of dinners and advice. She was beginning to know the area very well. She felt that by involving herself in the community she was not only demonstrating her desire, but somehow already living it.

Two months later, one of the homeowners invited her in as usual. This time, though, she was introduced to a lawyer who offered her the property for substantially less than it was worth. Several months later, Jasper moved into her newly purchased home.

Gerald was confined to bed. He demonstrated his "perfect health" by making up jokes. Every day he felt healthier and more energized until he felt ready to do something more to demonstrate "perfect health." He called comedy clubs and inquired about their requirements for bookings. He started recording his jokes. Several months later, Gerald's illness went into remission.

REFLECTIONS ON STEP FIVE
DEMONSTRATION

Demonstration is acting out in small, reasonable ways the things you have been picturing in your mind. Through demonstration, you integrate mind, soul and *body*.

Demonstration communicates to you, and to the universe, that you are truly ready to receive.

Demonstration is an outward and unreserved expression of belief, showing and cementing your faith.

Demonstration builds your imagination and increases your concentration. It expands your expectations, acceptance and love, promoting a positive outlook. It is an active form of visualization.

Demonstration is also a tool to quickly replace negative thinking with positive action during those times when the voice of diminishing intent threatens to steer you off course.

Consider the following suggestions as you engage in Step Five.

• Through demonstration, you are immersing yourself in possibility. Be alert and open to new ideas stimulated and received through demonstration. Guard against a narrowing of your focus.

For example, you expect a cake for your birthday from a friend, but being out of town that week, your friend sends you a gift certificate for an incredible bakery. Expecting a cake, you overlook the envelope in the mail, tossing it out with all your other junk mail. You're then left to wonder why your friend never sent anything.

We so often receive something much greater than anticipated. Watch for opportunity and the cues, signs and answers that will present themselves.

• Demonstration will train you to be more attentive to every interaction. Remind yourself that energy is working to place you amidst the people and events where it can quickly reproduce. Remind yourself that every conversation and interaction is another link in the energetic chain. Hold this awareness in your mind as you demonstrate. Listen and be attentive to your surroundings.

• The attentiveness you are gaining through demonstration will help you be more selective in what you let into your life. Keep in the forefront of your mind the importance of guarding your thoughts and energy.

Be selective in what you see and hear. Filter out information that isn't helping you. For example, television and radio imprint hundreds of images onto your consciousness in minutes, and these ideas repeat in your mind, acting as unnecessary clutter. Fill your mind with inspirational images and readings. Be attentive to what you listen to. Choose inspiring, uplifting music.

> Caress your consciousness with thoughts of things you love and enjoy.

Consider the people you choose to associate with and the events you choose to engage in. It's one thing to be gracious and kind, but we do ourselves no service when we continue to subject ourselves to energy-draining situations.

Recognize the events and people in your life that may be consistently draining your energy. We bring more benefit to more people when we fill and surround ourselves with love. Being drained again and again benefits no one.

The Bible holds this passage: "Give not that which is holy unto the dogs, neither cast ye your pearls before swine, lest they trample them under their feet and turn and rend you." (Matthew 7: 6)

Surround yourself with like-minded individuals and share.

As a note of caution, be mindful of telling others of your desires. People might say things like, "sure, okay, good luck with that" or "so, why hasn't it happened?" We can choose to disregard such comments, but in the moment negative words are spoken, they can interrupt the flow of energy. We are very much influenced by what we see and hear. A passing comment can be enough to plant a seed of doubt that begins to drain or deflect the energy we've worked to produce.

• Hold the idea of creativity in your mind as you choose your demonstrations. Be as inventive as you can. You might do something by phone or computer one day, then get out and visit some places and meet people on another day. Remember, every interaction is a link in the chain.

STEP SIX
manifestation

…Thought-Woman,
is sitting in her room
and whatever she thinks about appears.
—Leslie Marmon Silko, *Ceremony*

My divine energy, perfect substance,
flowing from my consciousness like a rushing current
into the physical world before me,
pools into perfect manifestation.

PRINCIPLES
ENERGY = MATTER

Manifestation is your dreams come true! It's the energy of your thoughts expressed on a level of physical awareness.

Einstein gave us the formula, $E=mc^2$, which perfectly describes how we can use the energy of our thoughts to manifest our desires. It tells us that energy is convertible to matter. In fact, all matter is simply a representation of energy and energy has mass—*energy* is the real and concrete substance that makes up our world.

The energy of our thoughts has its own materialization. It has substance or mass. It may be imperceptible to our senses, but it's no less real than energy we do see. And what we see and experience is simply more of the same substance.

Expressed another way, $E=mc^2$ parallels the metaphysical law, which states that all matter has its equivalent in mental energy and mental energy has its equivalent in materialized form.

Manifestation, then, is the end result of a systematic process, whereby energy is directed and accumulated toward a desired objective sufficient for it to be expressed on a level of physical reality.

HOW MUCH ENERGY IS REQUIRED
TO PRODUCE MATTER?

Einstein's revelation also tells us that it takes a large amount of energy to produce matter. In fact, we get a sense of just how much energy simply by looking at the formula, $E=mc^2$, which shows a measure of matter (m) multiplied by an incredibly large number (c^2), the square of the speed of light. So we know right away that it will take a comparatively large amount of energy to form matter, and when matter is converted, tremendous quantities of energy will be released.

We can see this relationship at work if we look up at the night sky. Stars consume matter and convert it into energy, and since a tiny amount of matter contains an extraordinary amount of energy, the stars we see tonight will still be burning millions of years from now.

With this understanding, you know that any time you make changes to the conditions of your life, energy is required, and the greater the change, the more energy that's needed. It makes sense then to expect that producing a greater desire will take more energy, though not necessarily more time.

The rate at which you manifest your desires is really a function of the quality of your thought energy. If your thoughts are strong, clear and uncluttered throughout the day, you continuously release enormous quantities of energy toward your desire. If your thoughts are scattered or frequently interrupted by negative thoughts, you release short, intermittent bursts of energy. And if you harbor competitive thoughts, you effectively short-circuit your efforts.

Think of the process of accumulating energy, like trying to fill a child's small outdoor swimming pool with a garden hose. If you direct the hose into the pool, turn the water on high and leave it there, the pool will quickly fill up. But if the hose falls out of the pool, becomes kinked or blocked, water is directed elsewhere, slows to a trickle or stops altogether. Meanwhile, much of the water already collected will evaporate.

Accumulating energy toward our desires is much the same as trying to fill a pool with water. If we want to manifest our desires quickly, we need to direct a steady stream of energy toward a desired objective, keep our thoughts and emotions elevated and see to it that our energy isn't blocked by clutter, deflected by distractions or stopped altogether by contradictory or competitive thoughts.

How Long Will My Desire Take To Manifest?

How quickly you achieve results depends on your ability to control your thoughts and emotions and use your powers of concentration and imagination.

Here are some questions to guide you in assessing the quality of your thoughts:

1. Upon rising in the morning, is your desire the first thing you see?

2. Do you immediately and purposefully fill your thoughts and emotions with a sense of belief, expectation and love?

3. Do you spend at least fifteen minutes a day concentrating on your desire and its details?

4. Do you consciously monitor your thoughts throughout the day, asking yourself from time to time, "What do I want to give myself in this moment?" Do you concentrate your efforts on the creation of your desire? Or are you, in small ways, harboring contradictory thoughts and emotions or carrying out actions injurious or harmful to your desires, your true self and the greater good?

5. Do you make a concentrated effort to replace destructive thoughts with productive images of your desire?

6. Do you purposefully take a few minutes each day—it doesn't have to be long—away from the hustle and bustle, to deliberately practice combining the steps and working with energy?

7. Do you spend at least five minutes a day demonstrating your desire? You can read about it or work on it or act in some small way in line with your desire. (Working on your collage or actively expressing your Trueprint is a great way to demonstrate.)

8. Before you fall asleep, do you state your desire, review its details and mentally program your thoughts to perform in the same way throughout the night?

THE KEY TO MANIFESTATION

The key to manifestation is to celebrate the gestation period of your desire, that time before its birth into the physical world.

It's so easy to become overly focused on the manifestation of your desire—what you see and touch—and forget that your desires already exist as a result of your thoughts, even before they manifest. When this happens, the process can become draining, because it's as if you're looking for a pair of glasses already atop your head; energy is wasted in a desperate and useless search for something you already possess. And though you work hard at the process and think positively about your desire, the energy you're generating is largely spent in anticipation of the material result, when it should be directed toward the result that already exists.

Celebrate the unseen reality of your desire. Wrap your thoughts around its details. Admire it. Cherish it. Wonder in awe at what is forming in the womb of creation and nourish it with your thoughts. Hold to the understanding that all matter has its equivalent in mental energy, just as all thought has its equivalent materialization. This understanding will lead you quite naturally to consistently celebrate the invisible that makes the visible possible. Manifestation will be an effortless, wondrous process.

MANIFESTATION IS AMAZING EVERY TIME

Every time manifestation occurs, it's amazing. It's one thing to agree to the truth of it, but it's something else altogether to "know" and experience this truth. Every time you manifest your thoughts, you know, in a familiar and concrete way, that you're a part of everything and every atom in the universe is listening and responding to you.

Every time you think, visualize or pray, you are speaking to the creative force in all things, the creative force that exists in every atom of your being. It's as if you're standing in front of a mirror speaking to your own reflection. So, instead of saying, "I need, I hope, I wish," say "This is what I will. I have faith in the power within me."

Remember that your every thought is a choice and every choice a new beginning. Purify your thoughts. Sacrifice your fear, anger and doubt on the altar of persistent striving, for a special wisdom is afforded those who regard every thought a choice and every decision a rebirth. Choose, and make holy the moment of your choosing, a re-dedication to the best of your being. Hold communion with your higher mind that you may speak to the highest, the truest and the best in all things.

Celebrate and express your purpose—choose your contributions and create. This life is truly your playground, your classroom, your gift.

METHOD
CELEBRATING

It's important to *celebrate* your power to manifest your desires. The dictionary defines celebration as doing something to show that a day or event is important, such as creating ceremonies or festivities to commemorate each thought. And this you have done!

You have already accomplished *Step Six* in the most significant way you can. The entire Practice is a repeatable series of rituals and ceremonies in celebration of the remarkable power within you. Living your life to its fullest

> Living your life to its fullest is the greatest gift to others.

is the greatest celebration of your gifts and achievements. It's the greatest gift to yourself and others.

Celebration, then, is the result of living all of the other steps in the Practice. And the more you apply the steps, the more your life becomes a celebration, for your life is a reflection of what you hold in the inner creative center of your being.

CELEBRATE ONCE A WEEK

Once a week, *demonstrate* the manifestation of your desire as though it has actually occurred, in some celebratory way. Celebrate for at least five minutes, though it can be much more if you like.

Invite friends over and throw a celebration party. Take someone to lunch or dinner specifically to celebrate. Purchase a celebration card for yourself and fill it out.

You might also treat yourself in some way. You could treat yourself to five minutes of peace and quiet wherein you don't answer the phone and you listen to your favorite music and relax. Or, enjoy a slice of chocolate cake or glass of wine. All the while, hold in your mind the awareness that you are celebrating the achievement of your desire. And experience what it feels like to be engaged in a small or grand celebration of your desire.

Also, this is five minutes wherein you take something for yourself. You have been learning through the Practice to open yourself to receive and the five minutes you spend to celebrate will help you to become even more comfortable with receiving— because for as much we say that we like to receive, it's surprisingly challenging

> If you would have something to give others, open and relish your gifts first.

for many of us. So, take a little something for yourself in celebration of the achievement of your desire. Buy yourself something. Let others take you out for a celebration. Spend at least five minutes engaged in some sort of festivity and fun that you truly enjoy, and celebrate your power, your desire—you! (And we will all benefit so much, you know that.)

CELEBRATE THE MANIFESTATION OF YOUR DESIRES

Each time you manifest one of your desires, acknowledge your achievement. If you are keeping a list of your desires, make it a ritual to cross off your manifested desires or place a checkmark beside them. Separate out the most significant related picture, word or symbol in your collage and frame it. Or take a picture of your actual achievement or use something that represents your success that you can hang up or display. This could be a check you have received, a letter of praise, the name of your first business client or some other item like a broken cigarette or a price tag.

You might also want to create a horizontal ladder, a piece of paper drawn with segments, to house each of your achieved desires. Each time a desire manifests, you can place it in your ladder. A horizontal display reminds you that no one desire is any more complicated to achieve than another. It reminds you that you have everything you need to create and it is only a matter of time before your desires are realized and you will fill the next segment of your ladder. In each unfilled section write: "*The answer is on its way.*"

It's important to display your achievement and create a ritual of appreciation for yourself, your gifts and the abundant universe. You might write a short thank-you note to your higher spirit or universal intelligence or record a message of celebration and appreciation for your gifts.

You might also wish to contact someone you know who needs assistance and give them some help. Or contact a charity or randomly assist someone when the opportunity arises over the next little while. This is a beautiful way to celebrate your gifts and create a ritual of thanks. It will remind you of your connection to others and outwardly express the miraculous qualities within you that make up your power to create.

This celebratory ritual of gratitude only needs to take a few moments. Sit in thankful silence, reflect and focus on the evidence of your creative ability. Acknowledge and revere the amazing power within you.

REFLECTIONS ON STEP SIX
MANIFESTATION

Manifestation is the energy of your thoughts expressed on a perceptible level. It's important to celebrate your ability to manifest your desires and also the achievement of your desires.

Here are some additional points to consider incorporating into your day.

• Write out the following, and occasionally read it or say it out loud: *"I am remarkable—infinitely so."*

• The next time you apply a step, just before you move on to something else, repeat the words of your Trueprint to celebrate your gifts and accomplishments. Or, you might like to come up with an additional word or phrase, such as, "It is done," as a way of celebrating and signifying the creation of your desires.

> For every miracle you see, you have shared millions you don't see.

As well, you will soon engage in the Practice unconsciously and you will be pleasantly surprised at how often you "catch" yourself applying the steps. For example, you may find yourself feeling irritated, but before you think too much about this you notice that you're looking for a pen, as your thoughts have turned to the detail of your desire.

In this moment, repeat your Trueprint or add a word or phrase to draw attention to the fact that you are celebrating. For example, Jenn says, "And so it is," reminding herself that what she thinks exists, and at the same time congratulating herself for a clear and consistent pattern of thought. Elena says, "I am so fabulous." The wonderful thing about the phrase, quote or word you choose, is that it is your own. You believe it and so it has strength. Thus, not only do you draw attention to the fact that you are celebrating, you caress your consciousness with energizing words and ideas.

This is a powerful tool. It's like putting a mental exclamation mark after your creations.

• Make a miracles list. Each day, write down the miracles and intriguing experiences you have throughout the day. Notice the small, miraculous "coincidences" that are occurring in your life and celebrate the manifestations of your gifts.

For example, Clair found herself a block away from her favorite bakery. So, she decided to buy herself a treat. She went in, spotted the treat she wanted, but then discovered she only had two dollars in her wallet. However, when she asked the clerk the price of the item, the clerk told her that it was on sale for fifty cents. Clair remarked, "That's great. I don't think I've ever been here for a sale." The clerk laughed and said, "I don't think I have either. Not two minutes ago, the manager marked down this item and it's the only item on sale!"

If you have started a small notebook to record the detail of your desires, you might leave a section at the end for keeping a miracles list and write in such events as they occur throughout the day.

When you make your list, realize that for every "miracle" and "coincidence" you see there are so many more that you don't. Celebrate the manifestation of your gifts and celebrate the many miracles you bring into so many lives, though you don't even know it.

• I feel compelled to state the obvious: be mindful of what you put into your body and how you treat your body. An excellent way to honor and celebrate your gifts is to care for the physical vessel that can increase or decrease the amount of energy you wield.

Please write out on a card, and place it where you can see it, perhaps on your fridge or exercise room, wherever you like: MODERATION, MODERATION, MODERATION.

Simply, be mindful of chemicals, such as alcohol and cigarettes, that deplete and drain your energy. Limit your intake of junk food, which makes your energy sluggish.

• You can quickly assess or *spot-check* your thoughts throughout the day to see if you are truly celebrating your gifts. Simply check to see if your thoughts feel fully creative, a feeling often described as a *click* in consciousness. Let me explain.

Say out loud, at a normal, relaxed pace, "I shall have an apple," or "I will have breakfast tomorrow." Take a moment to experience how this statement feels, how it resonates within your consciousness and body. Say it again and pay attention to the experience.

Now, in the same way state your desire. For example, "I will have a million dollars," or "I am manifesting a house, my desire is on the way." Does this statement feel the same as the simple declarative statement you made earlier? Or is there a sliver of doubt in your mind? Do you feel less sure about the truth of your desire statement?

When you think or say things like, "I will go out for lunch today," you don't think much about it. There are no doubts, fears or angers that suddenly well up and cloud your thinking. There are no heavy emotions working against your intentions or expectations. You know you're simply stating a fact.

It's this absolute "knowing" you want to feel when expressing your desire. This is often described as a *click* in consciousness when you know absolutely that what you are expressing is true. You are almost emotionally detached from the outcome, because it's simply a statement of fact.

Throughout the day, assess your thoughts to see if you are celebrating the manifestation of your desires. Check to see if you feel the same confidence, faith and truth in your creative statements that you feel in making a simple off-handed remark like, "I'll have dinner later," and if you do, you can be sure that your energy is elevated and effective and your desires are on their way!

sharing your practice

Earlier, we considered the importance of being selective in your associations. Just so, know that you can greatly enhance the process of manifestation by sharing your Practice and energy with one or several like-minded individuals.

IF TWO SHALL AGREE

It is eloquently expressed in Christianity, and stressed and reiterated in so many spiritual teachings around the globe, "That if two of you shall agree on earth as touching any thing that they shall ask, it shall be done…"

Let me share a story to make this clear. I spoke with a gentleman who was eager to apply for a promotion within his firm, but unfortunately, current policy prohibited him from applying as he lacked the required years of service and experience. I asked him to leave behind any negative thoughts and focus instead on what *should be* or more accurately, *what is*, as he would decide in his mind. I reminded him that the conditions of his life would shift around to allow him to experience the people, events and learning he willed to have in his lifetime. We talked for some time, and later that evening he sent an email applying for the position. Two days afterwards, he was granted an interview. He was one of only a few people out of hundreds to be selected. A little over a week later, he was given the position.

At this point, we met to discuss his next goal. He told me that the position he had just received was a stepping-stone. His ultimate goal was to move into what he called the "elite" team that handled really large projects. I asked him why. He said that in the elite team he would be working with very experienced individuals, learning a lot, and he could specialize in and focus on his interests.

I asked him what would have to happen for him to secure a position on the elite team. He said the position required more years of service. A number of individuals would have to retire to make room for new applicants and there would likely have to be a large project looming.

I quickly reminded him that requirements could change, as he had just demonstrated in securing his new role, and for the next several minutes we talked about what he would be doing on the elite team, what he would be learning and what it felt like to be a part of such a team. We both felt energized by the conversation.

The next day, the gentleman was called into a meeting and offered a promotion to the elite team. He was told that several people had chosen to retire and a large project was planned for the near future.

SHARING YOUR PRACTICE
WITH A PARTNER OR GROUP

You can share your Practice with another person or a group. In fact, as you progress in your own Practice, you'll be drawn to others they say *when the student is ready, the teacher will arrive.* And together, you'll discover new insights.

Others can assist you to identify and acknowledge your jailers, as they are somewhat more detached from your fears. They can point out when your words and actions are incongruent with your intentions.

You can talk about the details of your desire. Be sure to do so as if your desire is actually occurring. Talk about what you *are* doing and what it feels like to experience your desire. You can add each other's desires to your own list of desires.

You can visualize together. You might even like to take turns planning a visualization session and have the planner lead the group or other person through a guided meditation. You can plan to focus specifically on Step One, and work together to quiet your mind and body, acknowledge your thoughts and clear your mind. Another time, you might focus specifically on Step Three or work on passive visualization and cultivate your soul perception. You can share helpful ideas and techniques that have worked for you.

Remember, energy is not blocked or limited by walls or distance. You can share your Practice in absence, agreeing to visualize together, perhaps once a week, at a set time. And, do the same when working on your collage or detailing, focusing on both your desires or those of a group.

You can demonstrate together. You can go window-shopping or

research together. You can celebrate together! You can volunteer your time together in celebration of the manifestation of each other's desires.

Here are a few suggestions you might like to try:

CREATE A GROUP COLLAGE. You might like to divide up a poster board with equal space for each desire, then work together on one desire at a time, having each person add a picture, word, phrase, thought, symbol or item.

You will generate an abundance of energy with everyone focused toward the same objective.

SHARE YOUR WILL, BELIEF, EXPECTATION AND LOVE. Working with a partner, select a particular desire or area of life, such as work, partnership or spirituality and spend ten minutes detailing what you will, believe, expect and love for and about yourself.

Then, for the next ten minutes, write about the other person. Write out their desires and what you would choose for them. Write about what you think they should believe and expect for themselves. Write about what they should love about themselves.

When you're finished, share your responses. Note beliefs, expectations and loves that you find easy to express for another. You might discover yourself projecting your own desires. Pay attention to the energy, love and feelings being sent to you by the other person.

COMPLETE A GROUP TRUEPRINT. You can create a relaxing setting and complete a group Trueprint. Discuss the imagery, actions and meaning of each quality you choose. Afterwards, complete a project to express the qualities you define. Some ideas used by others include: quilting, jewellery, calligraphy and various other crafts. These can also be gifts that you give to others in celebration of the achievement of your desires.

Creating a group Trueprint is an almost meditative time where everyone's energy is focused on the source of creation. And it's time spent respecting yourself, being honest and forgiving.

Sharing your energy should never leave you feeling as though you are carrying something. You should always feel lighter.

HONOR YOUR HIGHER MIND. Create a relaxing setting; perhaps play some soothing music. Give each person a pen and paper and for ten minutes, write a letter of thanks to the energy of creation, your higher mind, source or essence.

PROJECT LOVE. For ten minutes, write a letter expressing your love for your partner or the others in your group.

You might agree to focus on a particular person and have everyone send love to that person. You might choose a particular group of people, which can be anywhere in the world. You might focus on the environment or animal kingdom. The important thing is that as a group, you generate feelings and expressions of love and focus them toward a particular objective.

Remember, you don't have to be assembled together to do this. You can set a specific time wherein you all agree to spend a few minutes projecting love to others.

You and a partner can set a specific time wherein you visualize sending love to the other. You will feel an increased energy during this practice. Use this time to work on seeing and feeling the energy you are projecting. Review the Principle of Creation and the active visualization session in Step Four and give energy imagery or sound.

If you are sending love to a specific person, you might record your love in an email or card that you can later mail to this person. You can do the same as a group.

You will see remarkable returns in your life by creating an outflowing of love.

Each time you align your energy with another, you speed the process of manifestation and encourage a more loving and joyous existence for all.

your beginning

This is a beginning. Whatever was is gone. *You are everything you need to be and everything you need is in you.* There is nothing beyond the power within you. You are capable of miracles. You are no different and have no less ability than the many others you've read about throughout this book who have achieved miracles. But you must *do.*

You must decide for those beliefs that most benefit your life and find your truth in doing—for it is in doing that we leap from rationality to understanding. Gautama Buddha said:

> *Distinguish between those who understand and those who agree. He who understands the Teaching will not tarry in applying it to life; he who agrees will nod and extol the Teaching as remarkable wisdom, but will not apply this wisdom to his life.*
>
> *There are many who have agreed, but they are like a withered forest, fruitless and without shade. Only decay awaits them.*
>
> *Those who understand are few, but like a sponge they absorb the precious knowledge and are ready to cleanse the horrors of the world with the precious liquid.*

You are on a path of understanding. The very fact that you are reading these words proves it. I urge you to act on the suggestions in this book. You have the steps to guide you further and the strength to follow them. What better time to start than now?

I want to thank you for every beautiful thought
that flows like a healing and purifying stream
through all our lives.

These words were received to be given as a benediction to many.
May you share them and grow in your own life
with each imparted blessing.

To order, visit:
www.professionaldreamer.com
or call toll free:
1-(8888)-1-1 MIND
1-(888)-811-6463

For more information on companion publications and
programs by Ghalil, including workbooks, coaching, seminars
and special events, or to find out about bulk purchasing
for individual, group, educational or charitable use,
or to share comments and experiences,
please visit:
www.professionaldreamer.com